Law Beyond the State

Law Beyond the State

Dynamic Coordination, State Consent, and Binding International Law

CARMEN E. PAVEL

OXFORD
UNIVERSITY PRESS

OXFORD
UNIVERSITY PRESS

Oxford University Press is a department of the University of Oxford. It furthers the University's objective of excellence in research, scholarship, and education by publishing worldwide. Oxford is a registered trade mark of Oxford University Press in the UK and certain other countries.

Published in the United States of America by Oxford University Press
198 Madison Avenue, New York, NY 10016, United States of America.

Library of Congress Cataloging-in-Publication Data
Names: Pavel, Carmen E., author.
Title: Law beyond the state : dynamic coordination, state consent, and binding international law / Carmen E. Pavel.
Description: New York, NY : Oxford University Press, [2021] |
Includes bibliographical references and index. | Contents: Hume's dynamic coordination and international law—Normative judgment, realism, and international law—The international rule of law—The compatibility of constitutional democracy and international law—Constitutionalism and pluralism : two models of international law.
Identifiers: LCCN 2020027364 (print) | LCCN 2020027365 (ebook) |
ISBN 9780197543894 (hardback) | ISBN 9780197543917 (epub) |
ISBN 9780197543924 (oso) | ISBN 9780197543900 (updf)
Subjects: LCSH: International law. | Constitutional law. | Rule of law.
Classification: LCC KZ3410.P383 2021 (print) | LCC KZ3410 (ebook) |
DDC 341.01—dc23
LC record available at https://lccn.loc.gov/2020027364
LC ebook record available at https://lccn.loc.gov/2020027365

DOI: 10.1093/oso/9780197543894.001.0001

9 8 7 6 5 4 3 2 1

Printed by Integrated Books International, United States of America

To my mom Ioana
Cu afectiune si gratitudine, acum si intotdeauna!

CONTENTS

FOREWORD

A few years back, at the start of this project, I was telling a colleague about a talk I was invited to give at another university. He asked what the talk was called, and I said, "Why Do We Need International Law?"

"Do we!?" he quipped sarcastically. I found this to be a common, albeit tactfully implicit, attitude among my colleagues in political science and philosophy. In these fields, international law is a relatively new, marginal subject. As distinguished from global justice, which has been getting increasing attention in political philosophy since the 1990s, or international relations, which has been on the radar of political scientists pretty much continuously since political science became a discipline, the rules and institutions of international law barely register as topics worth investigating.

I aim to change that. I am joining an energetic group of scholars working at the intersection of international law and political philosophy who highlight the important questions, dynamics, and effects of international law on states and individuals, such as David Lefkowitz, Jiewuh Song, Eva Pils, Steven Ratner, Andreas Føllesdal, Evan Fox-Decent, Evan Criddle, Fernando Tesson, Kit Wellman, Andrew Altman, Alejandra Mancilla, Samantha Besson, Allen Buchanan, and Leif Wenar. Their reasons for contributing to this emerging interdisciplinary field might be different than mine. My personal experience is that the more I learn about international law, the more numerous my reasons become. But chief among them are the following:

- International law is a very peculiar kind of law. If you ask, "peculiar in what way?," the answer depends on our models of law, which are largely inspired by the operation of law in domestic, state-based contexts. International law is illuminated by our conception of law built on these models, but it also raises fundamental challenges for them. International law is important because it requires us to consider with fresh eyes the question: "What is law?"
- International law also changes the relationship states have to each other, through rules about the use of violence, permissible conduct in war, the division of territorial boundaries, and the exchange of diplomatic representatives. By determining their physical boundaries, access to resources, and the limits of their legal jurisdiction, international law constitutes states as entities with legal rights and responsibilities that set limits on and shape processes of internal governance.
- Most fundamentally, international law also shapes the relationship that states have with their own citizens, so it matters to individuals in a "first-personal" way. International law regulates international travel, communication, mail services, trade in raw materials, food, and clothing. It sets limits on the permissible ways governments can treat their citizens and foreigners, regulates access to goods and services, and enables states in or impedes them from achieving domestic policy goals that affect the welfare of their citizens.

All of these facets of international law make it a fascinating topic for political philosophy, which is concerned primarily with how to justify the authority of legal and political institutions. This book contributes to this justificatory enterprise by turning its attention to the authority of international law over states. It addresses skeptics which hold that international law should not have any, or much, authority over states. But it asks further what kind of international law ought to have such authority. Therefore, the book is not simply a defense of the status quo, but takes a critical look at the ways in which existing rules of institutions may be defective from the standpoint of minimal requirements of justice and the rule of law.

This is a project that would not have started without the help and support of my good friend and mentor David Schmidtz and the staff, both academic and administrative, of the Center for the Philosophy of Freedom at the University of Arizona. They created an open-minded space and gave me the resources to go do my own thing, and for an academic there is no greater gift. The University of Arizona's philosophy community remains for me a model of welcoming, open-ended engagement, and of the serious, creative exchange of ideas. Graduate seminars were (and I am sure still are) famous as places that welcome all those interested, and the balance of students and faculty was fairly even. Everyone enjoyed the business of doing philosophy in a relaxed, jovial atmosphere, which often continued over drinks. People like Dave, Jerry Gaus, and many others created the kind of intellectual community that comes closest to a philosophical utopia. I am grateful to them and my colleagues in the Freedom Center—Dan Russell, Steve Wall, Guido Pincione, and Michael McKenna—as well as to the graduate students with whom I worked and formed lasting friendships, such as Chad van Schoelandt, Danny Shahar, Sarah Raskoff, Brian Kogelmann, Jeremy Reid, Lucy Schwartz, and many others. Some of them sat in my Philosophy of International Law class and were outstanding and engaging conversational partners. Most of all, thanks are due to Gayle Siegel and Rosie Johnson for keeping everything afloat with their professionalism—and lovely snacks.

I have been fortunate to move from one ideal intellectual community to another. My colleagues in the Department of Political Economy (DPE) at King's College London and in other parts of the college, particularly the Law School, have offered the essential intellectual support to refine and complete this project. DPE was started as an experiment ten years ago and is perhaps unique in the United Kingdom as a successful integrator of philosophers and political theorists, economists, and political scientists. In other words, it is a true Philosophy, Politics, and Economics utopia, which works not just because it was designed with this kind of interdisciplinarity in mind—it owes much to that—but because it nurtures some of the most thoughtful, able, imaginative, and fun academics I know, who genuinely value each other and add value to each other's work. A true measure of how lucky I feel to be their colleague is how much I miss spending time with them during this pandemic. I have been made to feel truly welcome at the Law School by John Tasioulas—who served until recently as the director of the Yeoh Tiong Lay Centre for Politics, Philosophy & Law—Eva Pils and her wonderful Human Rights, Development, and Global Justice seminar series, Ashwini Vasanthakumar, Lorenzo Zucca, Massimo Renzo, Leif Wenar, and many others. To them I owe the opportunity to engage on an ongoing basis with legal scholars and practitioners of international law, human rights law, international criminal law, jurisprudence, and legal philosophy.

I have presented this work before many audiences, all of whom have significantly shaped the final version. I thank the following audiences at these universities and events: the University of Arizona; the Global Constitutionalism conference at the National University of Singapore; the Brave New World conference at the University of Manchester; Legitimacy Beyond the State: Normative and Conceptual Questions Justitia Amplificata, Bad Homburg; The Political and Legal Theory of International Courts and Tribunals annual workshop PluriCourts, University of Oslo; University of Amsterdam workshop Should States Do It Alone? New Perspectives on the Legitimacy of Multilateral and Bilateral Power Structures; University of Hamburg; Cambridge University (Contemporary Political Theory Seminar Series); Oxford University (Nuffield Political Theory Workshop); McGill University (Legal Theory Seminar); University of Michigan Law School; University of East Anglia; Catholic University of Lisbon; UK-Latin America Political Philosophy Research Network Workshop; University College London; ECPR Joint Sessions Workshop; PPE Society Meeting; American Political Science Association Meeting; Eastern American Philosophical Association Meeting; and the ECPR General Conference.

The individuals who have listened to, read, and engaged with the ideas in this book are too numerous to list. But special thanks must go to Lucy Schwartz, Brian Kogelmann, Stephen Stich, Cord Schmelzle, Antoinette Schertz, Andreas Føllesdal, Patrick Taylor Smith, Terry Nardin, Steven

Ratner, Evan Fox-Decent, Omar Farahat, Catherine Lu, Steven Ratner, Annie Stilz, Kim Henningsen, Dan Bodansky, Peter Niesen, Markus Patberg, Dan Russell, Duncan Bell, John Filling, Cecil Laborde, Dario Maestro, Luke Wilson, Kate Powers, Michael Frazer, Christopher Meckstroth, Francisco García Gibson, Jiewuh Song, Oisin Shuttle, William Hasselberger, Ashwini Vasanthakumar, Eva Pils, Evan Criddle, Paul Sagar, and Robin Douglass. My students Tereza Rasochova and Alejandro Martin Rodriguez provided invaluable research assistance in the early stages of the project. David McBride was a patient and supportive editor at OUP, and the two anonymous referees made important suggestions on the last version of the manuscript. All my work is an attempt to meet the high academic standards set by my PhD adviser, John Tomasi. I am grateful to him for not lowering the bar.

Versions of chapters 1 and 3 of this book have appeared in print or online before. "Hume's Dynamic Coordination and International Law" appeared in *Political Theory* (forthcoming, online first), https://doi.org/10.1177/0090591720921831 (reprinted here with permission from Sage). "The International Rule of Law" appeared in *Critical Review of International Social and Political Philosophy* 23, no. 3 (2020), https://doi.org/10.1080/13698230.2019.1565714 (reprinted here with permission from Taylor & Francis). The first chapter has benefited from a John Templeton Foundation grant on "Philosophy, Politics, and Economics" while at the University of Arizona. The last two chapters have benefited from a John Templeton Foundation grant, project 60688 "The Ideal of Self-Governance," administered by the Center for the Study of Governance and Society at King's College London. I thank my former colleague Emily Skarbek and current colleagues Sam De Canio and Mark Pennington for facilitating it.

It seems so strange to publish a book during a pandemic, to believe that ideas still matter, and to have the luxury to consider the long-term health of our institutions, when other, more pressing issues loom so large. I am grateful for the love and support of my family and friends, particularly my wonderful children, Carla and Luca, who have sustained me during the last year with board games, meals cooked together, jokes, and lots of hugs. Jim's friendship, good cheer, and willingness to walk long miles with me have been invaluable through the last stage of getting the manuscript ready for publication. Finally, I dedicate this book to my mom, to whom I owe everything.

September 2020

Introduction

Law has a transformative potential. It can reduce conflict, protect rights, and facilitate cooperation. It emerges from the acceptance of the most minimal reciprocal limits on individual behavior, without which the simplest form of coexistence and interaction is not possible. Largely in incremental steps and sporadically in big leaps, law facilitates both the stability necessary for social cooperation and emancipatory transformation.

Does international law have this transformative potential? In this book I argue that it does. In the twenty first century, international politics is increasingly governed by legal rules and institutions. Large areas of international relations are shaped by treaties that are regularly renegotiated and updated to reflect the needs and interests of an evolving global community. Treaties governing the sharing of airspace for flight routes, the division of territory and territorial waters among states, the exchange of diplomatic officials, the trade of goods and services, and the treatment of citizens and foreigners are creating a dense mesh of international rules to which states commit, not always wholeheartedly. This ambivalence is the result of states' two conflicting impulses: on the one hand, the recognition that their own interests and autonomy are better protected by entering agreements which set limits on how other states behave, and on the other hand, the resolve to jealously guard their sovereign capacity to act unencumbered by constraints.

If grudging ambivalence is reflected in the external commitments of states, the writing of prominent scholars reveals far greater doubts about

Law Beyond the State. Carmen E. Pavel, Oxford University Press (2021). © Oxford University Press.
DOI: 10.1093/oso/9780197543894.003.0001

the project of building a robust system of international law. Widespread skepticism of its value and transformative potential, and sometimes outright hostility toward it abound (for a summary of recent views critical of international law, see Ohlin 2014; Sikkink 2017). International law is said to be in turn inconsequential to state behavior, the product of irrational state action which goes against national interest in a world of anarchy, or detrimental to the project of democratic self-determination. These attitudes pervade all corners of scholarly dialogue, insofar as scholarly dialogue takes up international law as a subject worth understanding and evaluating. Eric Posner's string of latest books aim to demonstrate the futility of international law when he says that "International law is [. . .] endogenous to state interests. It is not a check on state self-interest; it is a product of state self-interest" (Goldsmith and Posner 2005, 13). Due to the inherent inward-looking preferences of states, international law is incapable of creating order or solving collective action problems. Therefore we should maintain "a crisp analytic distinction between intrastate cooperation, which is capable of solving major nation-level collective action problems, and interstate cooperation, which is itself subject to collective action problems and thus cannot solve them, except in a very rudimentary fashion" (Posner 2011, 7). Posner is part of a new wave of legal scholars influenced by international relations realists, who are skeptical that the world can be explained in terms of anything other than raw power. Offering an ad hoc concoction of explanatory social science and normative analysis, realists such as Stephen Krasner say that "for realism, the central admonition for policy makers is that they must make prudent judgments. They must assess the consequences of their actions. They can never rely on moral precepts. Applying law and judicial proceedings to international relations reduces the likelihood of prudential calculations" (Krasner 2002, 267). This means in effect that states are better off ignoring the constraints of international law and may even be acting irrationally when they take them seriously. But skepticism is not just the purview of realists. More recently, Martha Nussbaum has claimed that international law is "leaching sovereignty away from the nation and its institutions, which are chosen by the nation's people, and turning it over to an international realm that is not decently accountable to people through their own political choices" (Nussbaum 2018). In Nussbaum's view, law can only be the product of a democratic community creating rules according to standards of accountably and inclusion, which can be obtained exclusively within states. To think law beyond states is possible and desirable is to imperil democratic self-governance and place hope in a false idol of order and justice.

These sweeping claims demonstrate the necessity of a normative justification for international law. This book provides that justification. My argument is straightforward: the same reasons which support the development of law at the domestic level—namely the promotion of peace; the protection of individual rights; the facilitation of extensive, complex forms of cooperation; and the resolution of collective action problems—also support the development of law at the international level. We are faced with multiple problems of order, justice, and cooperation beyond the borders of existing states: global warming, cross-border criminal activity, large-scale violations of human rights, health epidemics, failed states, wars, and refugees. Although some of these problems have been resilient due to timid and uneven efforts to address them, international law has made a significant dent in all areas of human cooperation and human rights.

The question of whether we need international law is parasitic on the question of whether we need law more generally. But it is importantly different. First, once we have a system or systems of law in place, as we do in most states except failed ones, it is not immediately clear that we need more law at the international level. More law is not always better. Therefore, international law needs its own justification. Second, the law governing the interactions of individuals and the law governing the interactions of states serve different purposes and have different functional properties. International law is made mostly by states setting standards of behavior among themselves. Currently it is made by states largely on a contractual basis, meaning that states are bound by treaties specifying basic rules of behavior at the international level only with their consent.[1]

Yet the reasons we might have for supporting a muscular, effective system of international law are not so different from the reasons which support developing law in general. Any justification of law must start with the recognition that there is no one single purpose it fulfils. But one of the most important among them is the creation and preservation of peace and order. The creation of social order out of chaos and conflict is an impressive human achievement. Law and legal institutions can limit the use of violence, allow individuals to live side by side in peace, and enable participation in common projects. Legal practice has evolved over a protracted, unfinished history of trial and error, in the shape of idiosyncratic, contingent institutional forms, and it has been marked by uplifting progress and discouraging regress. The most successful legal orders of our time encourage respect for individuals, inclusiveness, prosperity, innovation, and cooperation. The least successful are found in places where one's life and livelihood are at the mercy of opportunistic predators, insecurity and violence abound, and disease and poverty prevail.

Law can thus enhance the possibility of cooperation on a large scale, and it is against this assumption that we ought to understand and evaluate the genealogy and potential of international law. As the collection of bilateral and multilateral treaties, customary rules, principles and norms governing the interaction among states and the relationship they have with their own citizens, international law has yielded some impressive successes, which are left unexplained by those who question the viability of law at the international level. Among these successes are, the 1865 International Telegraphic Union; The Convention on International Civil Aviation (1944), also known as the Chicago Convention; the Declaration on the Granting of Independence to Colonial Countries and Peoples (1960); the United Nations Convention on the Law of the Sea (UNCLOS; 1982); and perhaps most surprisingly, the Montreal Protocol on Substances which Deplete the Ozone Layer (1989). The last of these has committed countries to eliminate the use of more than a hundred substances which have been shown to damage the ozone layer, it is the first treaty in the world to receive universal ratification, and as of 2010 it had achieved an astounding rate of compliance of close to 100% (Gillis 2018). These treaties represent a small cross-section of those which have helped states settle resource and border disputes, cooperate on international communication and travel, reduce the use of violence, increase accountability for the actions of states, and solve collective action problems. In fact, most international law is effective, but compliance rarely makes the news. What makes the news are examples of dramatic failure. Among them are the Kyoto Protocol, whose aim was to set binding emission reduction targets aimed at bringing global emissions at 5% below the level of 1990 emissions. The protocol is largely considered to have failed, due mostly to poor design of the rules and incentives (Clark 2012; Rosen 2015). The World Trade Organization (WTO) has now almost ground to a halt due to differences between member states about the terms of international trade and the procedures for negotiating and creating new rules. Crimes against humanity, war crimes, and genocide continue to be features of our political landscape, from South Sudan and the Democratic Republic of Congo, to Syria and Yemen, to Myanmar and North Korea, despite many human rights treaties proscribing them as international crimes.

While some of these failures are the result of poor design of treaty rules and enforcement mechanisms, many are the result of deep structural problems in international law, such as the outsized role state consent plays in creating rules and generating legal obligations. Take the practice of reservations for instance, which allows states to sign on to a treaty but opt out of certain provisions. The Vienna Convention on the Law of Treaties (VCLT, 1980) allows the use of reservations only to rules which do not constitute the "object and purpose" of a treaty (Article 19) and offers a byzantine system of reciprocal validation of state reservation by other state (Articles 20–23). Still, despite limits on the use of reservations and important advisory opinions from the International Court of Justice (ICJ), in the absence of binding procedures to judge whether certain treaty rules are essential to the "object and purpose" of a treaty, states are left to judge for themselves which reservations are permissible. The consequence of the lack of an authoritative mechanism is that states use reservations liberally and virtually unrestrained. Therefore, it is no accident that the article with the most reservations in the Genocide Convention (1951) is article 9, which gives jurisdiction to the ICJ over signatory states to ascertain whether the crime of genocide has been committed and to hold them accountable in case of direct involvement or failure to intervene in genocides occurring on their territory.[2] The implication of these sets of reservations is that states are left unable to interpret the full scope of the convention; to resort to authoritative, impartial judgments about violations of its rules; and to take action to prevent violations or hold perpetrators accountable. Ironically, one of the most common reservations to the VLCT is to Article 66, which also gives jurisdiction to the ICJ to settle disputes, thus removing any institutional capacity to properly interpret and limit the scope of reservations in international law. This kind of ambivalence illustrates what Andrew Guzman identifies as a "Frankenstein problem." States build international institutions to solve common problems, but out of fear of creating "monsters" with too much power, states are reluctant to give them real authority. The resulting institutions are not strong enough to solve the problems they were created for (Guzman 2013). This view challenges to some extent narratives about rational design of international agreements, which emphasize that states agree to what is rationally necessary for agreements to function well (Koremenos 2016).

This book responds to this ambivalence by offering moral and legal reasons for states to improve, strengthen, and further institutionalize the capacity of international law. The argument thus engages in institutional moral reasoning. It also shows why individuals should care that their states are part of a rule-governed international order. When states are bound by common rules of behavior, their citizens reap the benefits. States which accept limits on their behavior for the sake of international peace and justice will agree to not invade each other's territory, to reduce externalities from their domestic activities abroad, and to accept minimal standards of treatment for the people living on their territory. International law encourages states to protect individual rights and provides a forum in which they can communicate, negotiate, and compromise on their differences in order to protect themselves from outside interference and pursue their domestic policies more effectively, including those directed at enhancing their citizens' welfare.

A substantial and growing engagement with the morality of international law is emerging in the scholarly literature, but only indirectly with the normative justification of international law. The existing contributions can be classified into three approaches. The first approach provides general moral principles and values as standards of evaluation of international law and suggests reforms to bring international law in closer alignment with these principles and values. For example, Fernando Tesón discusses the conditions that states must meet to be accepted as participants with equal standing in international law and argues that states failing to respect basic human rights are not worthy of that status. States that are most likely to respect basic rights are liberal democracies, and he mounts a defense of the Kantian idea of a confederacy of free republics as the basis of a community ruled by international law (Tesón 1998, 3–22). Allen Buchanan asks what reforms of international law would make it more just, understanding the justice of international law as a condition of its legitimacy (A. Buchanan 2004, 5). He makes a case that to be just, international law must give effect to basic human rights, and unless it does so, it does not deserve our allegiance (A. Buchanan 2004, 118–90). Steven Ratner applies peace and compliance with human rights as minimal criteria for the evaluation of the justice of international law and provides a cautiously optimistic diagnosis of its current performance and future direction (Ratner 2015). Catherine Lu engages in a historically informed critique of the institutional practices of international law, many of which insufficiently acknowledge the harms of colonialism and do not make room for the demands of equality and inclusion by colonized peoples (Lu 2018). Evan J. Criddle and Evan Fox-Decent discuss a turning point in the evolution of international law that conditions the exercise of state authority on states' willingness and ability to satisfy a variety of fiduciary obligations with respect to their citizens (2016, 13–22). This sea change enables international law to better reconcile the tension between states' sovereignty and their obligations under international law (Criddle and Fox-Decent 2016, 94–106; Pavel 2015, 25–57). Jean Cohen and Turkuler Isiksel engage the growing focus on the constitutionalization of relations among states spurred both by the growth of international law and of sui generis entities such as the European Union (Cohen 2012; Isiksel 2016).

While these scholars are interested in whether the basic rules of international law meet certain requirements of justice, the second approach evaluates distinctive areas of international law from a philosophical perspective, such as international economic law, international environmental law, and international criminal law. For example, Leif Wenar has discussed the adequacy of the existing rules of international trade law and the extent to which they contribute to perpetuating relations of abuse and exploitation, particularly regarding the oil trade (Wenar 2016, 2015). Darrell Mellendorf and Simon Caney have focused on what are the appropriate ways to structure the burdens of preventing global climate change (Moellendorf 2014; Caney 2005). Andrew Altman, Christopher Heath Welman, Larry May, and Jamie Mayerfeld have discussed the boundaries and justification for international criminal law as well as the institutions that can interpret and enforce it (Altman and Wellman 2004; May 2005; Mayerfeld 2001). The first and second approaches are not mutually exclusive, as scholars engaged in the evaluation of the international legal system as a whole often draw prescriptions for specific areas of international law, such as secession or humanitarian intervention, as Buchanan and Tesón respectively do.

The third approach develops a more skeptical perspective and claims that international law has little or no authority over states. States engage in empty promises and cheap talk when creating common treaties, institutions, and rules, and the latter have negligible effects on how states ultimately act. Some realist international relations scholars go further to argue that it is imprudent for states to follow international rules even if they could change how states act (Waltz 1979; Mearsheimer 1994; Krasner 1999, 2002). Legal scholars such as Jack Goldsmith and Eric Posner have adopted the realist language to argue that international treaties constitute cheap talk, and that when states agree to international rules, they do not see themselves as accepting any external constraints on their behavior (Goldsmith and Posner 2005, 83–106; Ohlin 2014).

A skepticism apart can be inspired by the work of political theorists who defend loyalties to bounded political communities as a fundamental obligation, meaning that citizens should see themselves as giving priority to the demands of their political community over those of the international community (Stilz 2011; Miller 1997; Lefkowitz 2011). But no defender of this second kind of skepticism advocates a wholesale rejection of the authority of international law. Indeed, these moralized defenses of national loyalty are compatible with submission to general rules for states. The implication of these views is just that the balance should sway heavily in favor of state authority receiving the widest presumption for independence from outside interference, to give effect to the principle of democratic self-governance inside political communities. As such, moralized defense of the authority of states stand in sharp contrast to and should be separated from the radical skepticism of the value of international law inspired by realism.

Despite the wealth of recent work on international law, these three approaches either assume that the question about the reasons for asserting the authority of international law over states has been answered or deny that it is a meaningful question altogether, as representatives of realist skepticism do (Pavel and Lefkowitz 2018). The reasons for neglect in the wider philosophical literature reside in a lack of familiarity with international law and with the extent to which it governs so many areas which were previously considered exclusively the prerogative of sovereign states. This is understandable in an age of academic specialization in which combining two large fields of inquiry is limited by the need to master at least one field in order to maximize scarce professional opportunities. This book complements and extends the first two approaches by providing reasons to engage in international law building in the first place, and provides a set of reasons to reject the radical skepticism that informs some of the contributions to the third approach and to reconsider the right balance between obligations to states and obligations arising out of international rules characteristic of the moralized accounts of national loyalty.

Deep-seated skepticism that international law matters tends to dominate political and scholarly discourse and is fueled by the limits of theoretical models of orders developed in the context of sovereign states. Scholars and practitioners alike have difficulty imagining that the conditions of rule-governed social order can be met at the international level. Whether it is the possibility of meaningfully institutionalizing international law without resort to some global leviathan or the concern that to the extent that it will be institutionalized, it is likely to be an expression of powerful states' interests, understanding and evaluating international law amounts to an inconsequential distraction from the typical focus on the workings and legitimacy of domestic institutions and their attendant virtues and pathologies.

To understand why this kind of skepticism-fueled neglect misses a large part of the picture necessary to understand social order, we must appreciate the ways in which international law makes a critical, irreplaceable, and defining contribution to an international order characterized by peace and justice. Thus, the book has two distinct audiences. First, it speaks to those who are skeptical that international law can ever be more than an expression of powerful states' interests. It shows that properly conceived, states' interests require the development of a system of rules that allows them to protect themselves from each other's interference, resolve conflict, and engage in long-term cooperative behavior. Second, the book speaks to those who are persuaded by the transformative potential of international law. It shows that a commitment to international law as a framework of rules is more demanding than even its supporters realize.

THE PARADOX OF COMMITMENT TO LAW

Our inability to see the value and possibility of international law can be explained in part by a generalized belief that states will simply refuse to give away their autonomy in order to agree to be limited by common rules in their interactions. The acquiescence to constrain their own actions could be considered an abdication of their sovereign independence. Nonetheless, the difficulty of constraining one's freedom in order to enhance it is a well understood paradox of commitment in political science (Ferejohn and Sager 2002; North 1993; North and Weingast 1989; Holmes 1997; Isiksel 2016). The paradox is that "the ability to commit . . . expands one's opportunity set, whereas the capacity to exercise discretion . . . reduces it" (Shepsle 1991, 246).

James Buchanan called it the "paradox of being governed": "[M]en want freedom from constraints, while at the same time they recognize the necessity of order" (J. M. Buchanan 2000, xv). Rules preventing others from committing violence enable individuals to exercise moral agency and to act on their conception of the good life, namely to exercise their freedom. But rules also restrain freedom. Herein lies the paradox of law: to be free, we need to accept reciprocal restraints on our freedom. Only when such restrictions are reciprocal can we reap the benefits of a law-governed social order (J. M. Buchanan 2000, 136). The cost of being part of the social order is that one accepts constraints on oneself. Law reduces unwanted, unjustified interferences from others with our own freedom, and it requires that we in turn be similarly constrained in our behavior toward them.

Subsequent practical and theoretical advances have illuminated two levels on which this paradox exists. The first is the individual level, and it involves the difficulty of accepting constraints on one's freedom for the sake of greater freedom for all. Social contract theorists such as Thomas Hobbes, John Locke, Immanuel Kant, and Jean-Jacques Rousseau recognized this paradox and sought to explain why accepting the constraints imposed by law is an act of rational self-government (Hobbes 1994; Locke 1988; J.-J. Rousseau 1987; Kant 2017). By accepting the requirements of law, we become freer than before. The removal of physical danger and uncertainty from a world of absolute individual freedom creates space for individuals to plan their lives, to exercise their moral, mental, and physical capacities to the fullest, and it facilitates complex projects of social cooperation.

The second level obtains at the intrastate constitutional level, and it involves restrictions on the use of political power for the sake of institutional effectiveness. Turkuler Isiksel aptly documents the way constitutional politics reflects this paradox (Isiksel 2016, 41–45). Once kings began to accept the idea that they were bound by law, trust in the monarchy grew, and monarchy itself was reinforced, even while political power was divided through the multiplication of sites of authority (Holmes 1997; North and Weingast 1989). Although power was shifted away from the king and toward permanent legislatures and independent courts, formal institutional power grew. Rule-of-law restrictions on the authority of executive power have enabled an increase in the freedom of individuals subject to the law of the state and, crucially, of the other institutions in a state (Isiksel 2016, 42). For example, when the executive power is curtailed, it can interfere less with legislative power. Paradoxically, constitutional restrictions on the executive and other institutional capacities enable those capacities to be exercised with greater authority when they generate enhanced trust and a willingness to empower government with an expanded political mandate.

Although less recognized as such, this commitment paradox operates on a third level as well, namely in international politics. States continue to expect unlimited freedom in pursuing their own goals, yet their freedom to act is in fact limited dramatically when other states refuse to accept restraints on their actions. Absolute freedom for states in the international domain means freedom to invade one another, to pollute each others' waterways, to block access to essential transport routes, to refuse participation in solving collective action problems and providing public goods, and most importantly, to violate the rights of one's own citizens with impunity. Absolute freedom, or the more appropriate term for states, absolute sovereignty, leads to a world in which most states experience less freedom than they would under a rule-governed order, due to the ever-present possibility of interference into one another's affairs, heightened conflict and violence, and limited opportunities for complex forms of cooperation (Pavel 2015). When states agree to limit their sovereign discretion through international law, their freedom of action is protected and enhanced.

States have in fact already agreed to significant constraints on their behavior through customary law and international treaties. The most impressive example of voluntary restriction of sovereign authority is the multilevel integration of the European Union (EU). In agreeing to economic integration and cooperation with respect to cultural, social, and environmental policies, the members of the EU have transformed a situation "whereby the lack of constraints on sovereign power, particularly safeguards against cheating, gets in the way of sovereign's ability to exercise power effectively." The EU's supranational governance mechanisms can be best understood as a "commitment and monitoring device" (Isiksel 2016, 53, 53–55), which curtails some freedoms in order to enhance others.

The paradox of commitment through law illustrates the parallels between problems of rationality and cooperation at the individual level and those at the international level. Individual freedom and state sovereignty are twin relational concepts. Both have an internal and an external dimension. The internal dimension of individual freedom reflects the rational capacity of individuals to make choices governing their actions. The external dimension reflects the capacity to act on their choices without interference from others. Internal sovereignty reflects the rational capacity of states to govern themselves internally, often by granting final and supreme authority in matters of law and public policy to institutions operating on their territory. External sovereignty reflects the ability to exercise internal sovereignty without undue interference from other states or agents operating in international politics.

One of the arguments of this book is that just as individuals require external protections in order to exercise the internal dimension of their individual freedom, so too states cannot exercise internal sovereignty unless their external sovereignty is protected, and such protection depends on a strong, authoritative, efficacious system of international law. The fundamental rules of mutual tolerance among states are not self-enforcing. States require institutionalized, impartial mechanisms for interpreting, applying, and enforcing those rules, as well as for solving the inevitable conflicts and disagreements that arise in the process of deciphering and complying with them.

I will show that one of the tried and tested ways to solve the paradox of commitment, namely constitutionalism, can offer important lessons for building a more robust system of international law. Constitutional agreements have created precommitment mechanisms for individuals and political officials by asking them to agree to second-order rules and principles (rules about rules) to guide the making of first-order rules of behavior. They have not always taken the form of explicit constitutional agreements, and the commitments have been incremental and tacit more often than not. I argue that constitutionalization is necessary for states to express their commitment to the common project of international law. This argument is built on the recognition that although in the case of specific decisions, states may wish to act uninhibited by external constraints, in the long term they will all benefit by a set of mutual restrictions that temper the temptation to act unconcerned about the effects of one's actions on others. Among states, just as among neighbors, rules protecting freedom must coexist with rules restricting freedom. And it is important to be specific about what those protections and restrictions will entail, in a manner that elicits some precommitment both to solving disagreements via rules (a constitutional commitment) and to specific protections and limitations on states' freedom to act.[3]

Constitutionalization does not get off the ground without the acquiescence of the most powerful actors in the system. Constitutionalization of domestic law is not possible without the voluntary acceptance of constitutional restraints by the executive and other powerful public and private authorities, and it will not be possible at the international level without the participation of the most powerful states. The process of constitutionalization of international law is further complicated by additional principal-agent problems; the interests of citizens living in different states in constraining their own states, both with respect to each other and their own citizens, do not always align with the interests of the political officials who represent them. Yet this merely replicates on a different scale what is already a principal-agent problem of political institutions at the domestic level; it does not introduce a new one. The executive, legislative, and judiciary in a domestic constitutional order also represent the interests of their citizens imperfectly. Despite the attendant difficulties, some constitutional orders, namely those in liberal democratic societies, have been quite successful in limiting the discrepancy between principals and their agents, although they have not eliminated it. Their experiences can teach us about the processes, safeguards, and substantive rules which a constitutional order must enact at the international level in order to be effective.

International law is not yet constitutionalized, but it has created a number of formal institutions and organizations with powers to make, apply, and enforce rules. Its progressive institutionalization leaves significant gaps and structural deficiencies, such as an overreliance on state consent, and rules that privilege the powerful states and shield them from accountability for their actions. States cannot be bound by international treaties without their consent, which means for instance that criminal responsibility under the jurisdiction of the International Criminal Court (ICC) continues to be quasi-optional (it is non-optional only with Security Council referral), as are most of the rules of international law, with the important exception of customary law and the rules of the United Nations Charter. Fixing those gaps and deficiencies is what makes the project of developing international law demanding.

WHY NOT A POLITICS OF INTERNATIONAL ANARCHY?

While Thomas Hobbes has made immeasurable contributions to political philosophy, he has perpetually confused and misled international relations scholars. Hobbes posited a stark dichotomy between a lawless, anarchic state of nature, in which violence and uncertainty make life "solitary, poor, nasty, brutish, and short," and a state of law and security achieved under an absolute monarch, a leviathan (Hobbes 1994, 76). In the state of nature, Hobbes argued, it is irrational for individuals to observe restrictions on their own behavior while having no assurance that other individuals will do the same. This will only expose those who follow natural law to the predatory actions of others who will stop at nothing to gain a relative advantage and satisfy their thirst for power and glory (Hobbes 1994, 99–100). The most important problems in the state of nature are those of assurance and trust, and the way for individuals to solve those problems is to commit reciprocally to institutional mechanisms designed to alleviate them. Yet what many miss is that the state of nature was never intended and does not function in Hobbes's political philosophy as a description of an actual stage of human development, but rather serves as a hypothetical device meant to explain the rationality of committing to and respecting a system of law (Waldron 1994; Williams 1994). Hobbes used the state of nature as an instrument for showing the importance of reciprocity in human affairs bound by effective commitments, as well as the necessity of respecting legal institutions that secure widespread compliance with rules.

However, the dichotomy Hobbes posited continues to influence countless international relations scholars, especially realists, who believe that since we do not have a functioning global leviathan, what we are left with is by necessity an international state of nature, in which every state is preoccupied exclusively with its own survival at the expense of every other state. International anarchy is a condition of limited and fragile cooperation, because engaging in cooperation with other states exposes one to cheating, renders one vulnerable to exploitation, and ultimately threatens one's survival. This explains the recurring and rather simplistic insistence that states are preoccupied with "relative gains," which means that they are prone to engage in exchanges with other states only if they are bound to gain more relative to other states (Mearsheimer 2001, 1994; Grieco 1988; D. L. Rousseau 2002).

Commonly described as the realm of lawless anarchy, from which there is no possible escape, international politics is condemned to a limited and unsatisfactory range of solutions to the ongoing threat of conflict and violence: a military balance of power, a hegemon which sees preserving some measure of international peace in her own interest, or a global leviathan. The first two of these are more temporary and unstable, since they are undermined by changes in the military fortunes of the dominant states, and the last is unlikely. Therefore, realists believe that a rule-governed order is simply not possible in international politics beyond the rudimentary rules which dominant states are willing to impose and support to maintain their power. In prominent corners of political science, international law is not taken seriously as a tool able to bring about coordination, cooperation, and stable peace and justice.

However, Hobbes taught us that there are distinct but related structural problems in anarchy that are worth considering:

1. The problem of lack of rules to remove the prospect of ongoing conflict, "a war of all against all." This problem obtains when expectations of behavior are not clear and there are no authoritative mechanisms in place to either make new rules or interpret, apply, and enforce existing rules. These are first-order problems of assurance and trust.
2. The problem of a lack of commitment to second-order rules about making primary rules of behavior that solve first-order problems of assurance and trust.

Luckily, the development of international law has both outpaced and outpredicted the theoretical models used to characterize international politics as a war of all against all. States now rely on a fairly sophisticated and institutionally differentiated system of international law which ameliorates both first-order problems of assurance and trust and second-order problems of commitment, though imperfectly. This encouraging evolution of international cooperation shows that David Hume, rather than Thomas Hobbes, is a better guide to understanding the problem of order at the international level.

Individuals leave the Hobbesian state of nature as soon as they develop rules of interaction on a small scale. Rules emerge when individuals begin to adjust their behavior toward others in a process of dynamic coordination, often in response to conflict. At first rules arise as social conventions in small, kin-based communities, and then they spread outward as communities develop dense networks of interaction with each other (Hume 2000, 307–64; Sabl 2012, 6). Social learning takes place as rules extend their area of applicability, as both individuals and communities experiment with different solutions to problems and adapt to each other. Although initially driven by self-interest, individuals come to respect the interests of others and to give them a place in their own conception of what a good social order looks like (Frazer 2012, 78; Sabl 2012, 49–50). Eventually the benefits of conventions spread equally to all individuals through institutionalized systems of rules, namely through laws made by sovereigns, aided by impartial application by magistrates (Hume 2000, T3.2.7.7).

Section XI of the *Treatise on Human Nature on the Law of Nations* illuminates the similarity and complementarity Hume saw in domestic and international law. The needs of individual persons and states for social coordination are analogous in Hume's view: "[A]nd indeed this assertion is so far just, that different nations, as well as private persons, require mutual assistance; at the same time that their selfishness and ambition are perpetual sources of war and discord" (T 3.2.11.1). We can indeed draw parallels between dynamic coordination among individuals through domestic law and that of states through international law. Informal conventions have arisen via customary international norms that have allowed states to coordinate expectations in areas essential to their interactions, such as the exchanging of ambassadors, the treatment of each other's citizens, and the regulation of trade. International law has moved more decisively past a Hobbesian state of nature with the creation of formal multilateral treaties, whose role is to balance conflicting interests and assign rights of way among states.

If international politics is better understood as a Humean social order ruled by complex conventions rather than a lawless state of nature, it remains true that existing conventions are precarious without a stronger commitment to international law as a shared, global project. The existing second-order rules about how to make primary rules of behavior, such as those embodied in the VCLT, are weakly institutionalized and occasionally ambiguous. Structural weaknesses in international law have several important consequences. States continue for the most part to be judges in their own cases, while the inability of international courts to exercise compulsory jurisdiction exemplifies and amplifies the problem of commitment and trust. Without substantial reform, including strengthening the rule of law requirements such as equality before the law, accountability for the violation of legal obligations, and courts with compulsory jurisdiction, international law cannot offer the benefits that states have good reasons to pursue.

FEASIBILITY AND EFFECTIVENESS

Legal scholars, political scientists, and political philosophers alike tend to raise questions about the feasibility of substantive institutional reform. Concerns about feasibility are legitimate and necessary. Nonetheless, calls for resisting reform at the international level are often grounded in a mistaken belief in the immutability of states' preferences. These preferences often reflect opposition to international cooperation and to the necessity of strengthening international law. Critics believe that since states do not favor these changes, such changes are not feasible. But a major weakness of this approach is to assume that preferences are fixed. Nonetheless, when states express a lack of interest in specific projects of international law creation and in more ambitious projects of structural transformation, as they often do, such positions, even when long-standing, can be subject to persuasion, reconsideration, dialogue, and compromise due to pressures both internal and external. Indeed, this was Hume's enduring lesson. Dynamic interaction among states results in a process of adaptation, learning, and change, including changing in states' self-understanding of their preferences and interests. If this were not true, we would not see anywhere near the level of development of international law that we see today. States have been persuaded time and again about the benefits of substantive and radical transformation of the international order, including the creation of the United Nations, decolonization, trade agreements, human rights and humanitarian law.

Therefore, we need to examine more closely the claim that a given proposal is feasible or infeasible. Due to space constraints, I am not able to engage this claim here, but I would like to preempt a few concerns from those who label institutional proposals for reform at the international level "infeasible." One worry I have about talk of feasibility is that we often take it as an extrinsic feature of the world, apart from the beliefs and norms agents develop to cope with ongoing problems or a changing reality. That is, we often think of feasibility as an exogenous feature of agents' preferences. But feasibility is to an important extent endogenous. It depends on beliefs and commitments, and scholarly research can play a role in changing the beliefs, norms, and preferences of those operating as agents of change in international politics and law.

Anytime a proposal for substantive institutional transformation in international politics is put forward, people understandably feel uneasy about the risks involved or are discouraged that a critical mass of states is not likely to sign on. Concerns about feasibility are introduced often as a conversation stopper. They should be anything but. Consider the many changes characterizing the evolution of international law in the past eighty years. Many of them would have seemed to contemporary observers as utopian and infeasible as few as five to ten years before they took place. Were the creation of the United Nations and the UN Charter feasible in 1940? Was decolonization feasible in the late 1940s? Was the Montreal Agreement for the Protection of the Ozone Layer, one of the most successful international treaties in terms of membership and compliance, feasible in 1970? The answer to all of these questions is probably "no." These changes were brought about by significant pressures from domestic interest groups, international nongovernmental organizations (INGOs), committed states, and long processes of negotiation among and socialization of state officials. Invariably these processes brought about changes in the preferences and perceived interests of a critical mass of international diplomats and state representatives, without which none of the successive treaties would have gotten off the ground.

Therefore, while concerns about feasibility are necessary, they are not persuasive when they take the form of "states will never agree to this kind of reform." States may or may not agree, and I see my role as providing reasons for states to change their preferences toward developing a stronger, more effective system of international law. I do so by providing arguments whose aim is to change states' perceptions of what a decent, mutually advantageous, morally acceptable international law order should look like.

A version of this concern with feasibility is that big powers will never agree to reform because it is not in their interest to constrain their power more than they already have. This may be the case, and prediction is not the strong suit of political philosophy. But states have already agreed to constrain their power through a variety of international treaties and institutional mechanisms, so the question arises: Why is this particular equilibrium we have achieved in international law today of constraint versus freedom the one we should stick to? States have in the past acted on good reasons to restrain absolute sovereignty in a variety of areas of international politics, and as I will show, we have not run out of reasons to implement further limitations via structural changes.

Big powers have willingly participated in this transformation and have taken entrepreneurial roles to guide reform at different historical moments. The United States has been a strong proponent of a more muscular and effective dispute resolution mechanism in the WTO (Goldstein and Gowa 2002; Goldstein and Steinberg 2008; Elsig 2017). The International Monetary Fund (IMF) and the World Bank have extended voting rights to developing countries as a result of the agreement of the small number of powerful member states with voting rights to dilute theirs in order to enhance the legitimacy and quality of these organizations' decisions (BBC News 2015). And of course, European powers have agreed to significant transformation of their sovereignty in becoming members of the EU (Weiler 2003; Bellamy 2017; Isiksel 2016). I advocate nothing as substantive as a EU-style pact at the global level, but rather the recognition that having an effective legal system requires a serious commitment to a constitutional framework and rule-of-law values, without which international rules can be made neither binding nor legitimate.

Another version of this concern with feasibility, which I address more extensively in chapter 4, is based on worries about subordinating domestic interests to an international institutional order. My argument is that a partial subordination is necessary if states are to reap the benefits of the protection which international law offers to them and their citizens. Limiting the means that states employ to achieve their objective and insisting that their objectives be legitimate and compatible with the objectives of other states is a requirement of a peaceful, rule-governed order. Torture, crimes against humanity, and interference with other states are among the limitations on states that would be embodied in a global constitutional order. These norms are already part of international law, but to give them constitutional level protection means to institutionalize a qualitatively different hierarchical and non-consensual status for them over state sovereignty.

Showing that structural reform at the international level is feasible in principle because states' preferences for cooperation might change does not answer other important questions, such as how to encourage states to build the political will to negotiate and accept a constitutional pact. I see the purpose of this book as providing reasons for them to believe that one such pact is needed. Much else is required to persuade states to do it. Diplomatic efforts, transnational advocacy, and local citizen mobilization are some of the tools of those trying to implement reform. This book lays the groundwork for a different framework for understanding, evaluating, and critiquing the international order and derives blueprints for reform. Only when these blueprints are in turn taken up, evaluated, transformed, and adapted into a new language and justification for action by norm entrepreneurs, activists, and political representatives will the book have made a difference.

STRUCTURE OF THE BOOK

Chapter 1 argues that states cannot have it both ways: they cannot reap the benefits of a system of international law that ensures predictability, sets limits on the permissible ways they can treat each other and their citizens, and ultimately guarantees a sphere of autonomous state action, and at the same time claim that international law is optional and their autonomy absolute. Building on David Hume's model of dynamic coordination, I provide a moral justification for the necessity of developing international law with distinctive rule-of-law features. The implication of this justification is that we must strengthen the essential features of international law that allow states and individuals to reap the benefits of its protections, such as nonoptional rules that articulate a moral minimum, courts with compulsory jurisdiction, and stronger mechanisms of enforcement.

Chapter 2 engages a distinctive type of skepticism of international law found in the writings of international relations realists and those outside of international relations whom they have influenced. Like other social scientists, realists draw lessons for policy makers from their theories. They tend to advise that breaking the rules of international law is acceptable or even required when those rules conflict with a state's interests. Yet the fact that realists have attitudes about what states should or should not do requires at least prima facie an explanation. As social scientists, realists seek to produce explanatory theories about how (state, nonstate, and international) institutions act, not how institutions *should* act. They build a picture of how states act by relying on rational choice. The model of the rational egoist, initially developed for predictive purposes in economics, has proven to be a highly successful tool for modeling the behavior of individual and collective agents. My aim in chapter 2 is to explore both the ways in which realists draw normative judgments from factual assumptions about the nature of international politics and the types of unarticulated moral assumptions that help them get there. I show that realists' prescriptions about states' attitudes toward international law stem from deploying the rational choice model applied to states *prescriptively* rather than merely *descriptively*.

Chapter 3 asks whether the ideal of the rule of law has a place in international law. There is wide agreement that the decentralized and consensual nature of international law and the paucity of dispute resolution forums and administrative and enforcement organs means that domestic rule-of-law requirements cannot be simply transplanted to the international realm. For example, it is more difficult to identify the public officials in international law whose arbitrary power must be restrained. The requirements of an international rule of law must be interpreted and specified for the very different context of international law. I argue that one of the main goals of an international rule of law is the protection of individual and state autonomy from the arbitrary interference of international institutions, and that the best way to codify this protection is through constitutional rules restraining the reach of international law into the internal affairs of a state. State autonomy does not have any intrinsic value or moral status of its own. Its value is derivative, resulting from the role it plays as the most efficient means of protecting autonomy for individuals and groups. Therefore, the goal of protecting state autonomy from the encroachment of international law will have to be constrained by, and balanced against, the more fundamental goal of an international rule of law—the protection of the autonomy of individual persons—best realized through the entrenchment of basic human rights. Based on this understanding of an international rule of law, I begin to build a case for the constitutionalization of international law.

Chapter 4 shows that the principle of national constitutional supremacy sits uneasily with the authority claimed by international law to constrain state action, even action arising in conformity with constitutional rules. The fact that national constitutions and international law claim to regulate the actions of states need not necessarily be a problem. States perform many actions that are outside of the purview of international law. However, as international law has steadily expanded into areas previously considered the exclusive legal prerogative of sovereign states—such as tax rates for imports and subsidies to domestic producers, environmental protection, control over territorial waters, and the treatment of citizens and foreigners residing on their territory—the possibility of clashes between the authority of domestic and international law has increased, as states' obligations under international law can come into conflict with the obligations they incur under domestic law. For example, a country can authorize via parliamentary action a war against another state in accordance with its constitutional rules, yet the rules of the UN Charter can prohibit that war as detrimental to international peace or as an unjustified interference with the sovereign authority of another state. The executive can demand increased tariffs on foreign imports in violation of WTO rules which require that negotiated tariffs remain at agreed levels.

Compared to ordinary violations of the law in which weak-willed or ill-meaning agents fail to fulfill their obligations, violations of international law stemming from the demands of constitutional supremacy are qualitatively different. The authority of various institutions in a constitutional democracy is democratically sanctioned, which comes with a special moral force and normative legitimacy. Even when these institutions make decisions which undermine international law, they are often seen as a legal and perhaps moral expression of collective self-government. Therefore, one of the unappreciated features of constitutional supremacy is its democratically sanctioned potential to subvert international law and ultimately weaken the protection it affords to states and to the rights and interests of their citizens. I argue that this incompatibility is real, but it is only a contingent feature of the relationship between existing constitutional democracies and international law. It can be reduced or resolved by changes in rules at both the domestic and the international levels, and I suggest that a form constitutionalization of international law does the least possible damage to domestic constitutional supremacy while reconciling it with central demands of international law.

Chapter 5 defends constitutionalism against views that require the preservation or scaling back of the current institutionalization of international law, most notably legal pluralism. Legal pluralism consists of a descriptive and normative view. The descriptive view represents the international realm as a contest of overlapping legal systems, including state, regional, and international law, without any one having supremacy in cases of conflict. The normative view portrays efforts to tame legal pluralism within the constraints of a constitutional order as doing an injustice to legitimate political and social differences. According to legal pluralists, legal conflict among the claims of various communities is unavoidable in a world marked by legal pluralism, but it is also desirable insofar as it preserves the values inherent in various legal systems and refrains from stifling moral, social, and legal diversity through the imposition of narrow hierarchies. The arguments I offer show why pluralism fails as a normative ideal of international law. I defend the advantages of a constitutional hierarchy over legal pluralism. Importantly, I show that constitutionalism can preserve to a large extent the pluralism inherent in international law but also corrects its most important failings, namely legal uncertainty and indeterminacy, lack of commitment from states for a rule-based order at the international level, and the proliferation of deeply oppressive and unjust state legal orders. Finally, I explain why, despite existing arguments to the contrary, the

UN Charter does not meet the standards of an adequate constitutional treaty for international law.

REFERENCES

Altman, Andrew, and Christopher Heath Wellman. 2004. "A Defense of International Criminal Law." *Ethics* 115 (1): 35–67.

BBC News. 2015. "IMF Reforms Clear Last Hurdle." December 19, sec. Business. https://www.bbc.com/news/business-35141683.

Bellamy, Richard. 2017. "A European Republic of Sovereign States: Sovereignty, Republicanism and the European Union." *European Journal of Political Theory* 16 (2): 188–209. https://doi.org/10.1177/1474885116654389.

Buchanan, Allen. 2004. *Justice, Legitimacy, and Self-Determination: Moral Foundations for International Law*. New York: Oxford University Press.

Buchanan, James M. 2000. *The Reason of Rules*. Vol. 10. Indianapolis, IN: Liberty Fund.

Caney, Simon. 2005. "Cosmopolitan Justice, Responsibility, and Global Climate Change." *Leiden Journal of International Law* 18 (4): 747–75.

Clark, Duncan. 2012. "Has the Kyoto Protocol Made Any Difference to Carbon Emissions?" *Guardian*, November 26, sec. Environment. https://www.theguardian.com/environment/blog/2012/nov/26/kyoto-protocol-carbon-emissions.

Cohen, Jean L. 2012. *Globalization and Sovereignty: Rethinking Legality, Legitimacy, and Constitutionalism*. Cambridge, UK: Cambridge University Press.

Criddle, Evan J., and Evan Fox-Decent. 2016. *Fiduciaries of Humanity: How International Law Constitutes Authority*. New York: Oxford University Press.

Elsig, Manfred. 2017. "Legalization in Context: The Design of the WTO's Dispute Settlement System." *British Journal of Politics and International Relations* 19 (2): 304–19. https://doi.org/10.1177/1369148117690890.

Ferejohn, John, and Lawrence Sager. 2002. "Commitment and Constitutionalism." *Texas Law Review* 81: 1929.

Frazer, Michael L. 2012. *The Enlightenment of Sympathy: Justice and the Moral Sentiments in the Eighteenth Century and Today*. New York: Oxford University Press.

Gillis, Justin. 2018. "The Montreal Protocol, a Little Treaty That Could." *New York Times*, October 19, sec. Science. https://www.nytimes.com/2013/12/10/science/the-montreal-protocol-a-little-treaty-that-could.html.

Goldsmith, Jack L., and Eric A. Posner. 2005. *The Limits of International Law*. New York: Oxford University Press.

Goldstein, Judith, and Joanne Gowa. 2002. "US National Power and the Post-War Trading Regime." *World Trade Review* 1 (2): 153–70. https://doi.org/10.1017/S1474745602001131.

Goldstein, Judith L., and Richard H. Steinberg. 2008. "Negotiate or Litigate? Effects of WTO Judicial Delegation on U.S. Trade Politics." *Law and Contemporary Problems* 71 (1): 257–82.

Grieco, Joseph M. 1988. "Anarchy and the Limits of Cooperation: A Realist Critique of the Newest Liberal Institutionalism." *International Organization* 42 (3): 485–507.

Guzman, Andrew. 2013. "International Organizations and the Frankenstein Problem." *European Journal of International Law* 24 (4): 999–1025.

Hobbes, Thomas. 1994. *Leviathan: With Selected Variants from the Latin Edition of 1668*. Edited by Edwin Curley. Indianapolis, IN: Hackett Publishing.

Holmes, Stephen. 1997. *Passions and Constraint: On the Theory of Liberal Democracy*. New ed. Chicago: University of Chicago Press.

Hume, David. 2000. *A Treatise of Human Nature: Being an Attempt to Introduce the Experimental Method of Reasoning into Moral Subjects*. Edited by David Fate Norton and Mary J. Norton. New ed. Oxford: Oxford University Press.

Isiksel, Turkuler. 2016. *Europe's Functional Constitution: A Theory of Constitutionalism Beyond the State*. Oxford: Oxford University Press.

Kant, Immanuel. 2017. *Kant: The Metaphysics of Morals*. Edited by Lara Denis. Translated by Mary Gregor. 2nd ed. New York: Cambridge University Press.

Koremenos, Barbara. 2016. *The Continent of International Law: Explaining Agreement Design*. Cambridge, UK: Cambridge University Press.

Krasner, Stephen D. 1999. *Sovereignty: Organized Hypocrisy*. Princeton, NJ: Princeton University Press.

Krasner, Stephen D. 2002. "Realist Views of International Law." *Proceedings of the Annual Meeting (American Society of International Law)* 96 (March): 265–68.

Lefkowitz, David. 2011. "The Principle of Fairness and States' Duty to Obey International Law." *Canadian Journal of Law and Jurisprudence* 24 (2): 327–46.

Locke, John. 1988. *Two Treatises of Government*. 3rd ed. Cambridge, UK: Cambridge University Press.

Lu, Catherine. 2018. *Justice and Reconciliation in World Politics*. Reprint ed. Cambridge, UK: Cambridge University Press.

May, Larry. 2005. *Crimes against Humanity: A Normative Account*. Cambridge, UK: Cambridge University Press.

Mayerfeld, Jamie. 2001. "The Mutual Dependence of External and Internal Justice: The Democratic Achievement of the International Criminal Court." *Finnish Yearbook of International Law* 12: 71–107.

Mearsheimer, John J. 1994. "The False Promise of International Institutions." *International Security* 19 (3): 5–49.

Mearsheimer, John J. 2001. *The Tragedy of Great Power Politics*. New York: W. W. Norton.

Miller, David. 1997. *On Nationality*. New York: Oxford University Press.

Moellendorf, Darrel. 2014. *The Moral Challenge of Dangerous Climate Change: Values, Poverty, and Policy*. New York: Cambridge University Press.

North, Douglass C. 1993. "Institutions and Credible Commitment." *Journal of Institutional and Theoretical Economics (JITE)/Zeitschrift für die Gesamte Staatswissenschaft* 149 (1): 11–23.

North, Douglass C., and Barry R. Weingast. 1989. "Constitutions and Commitment: The Evolution of Institutions Governing Public Choice in Seventeenth-Century England." *Journal of Economic History* 49 (4): 803–32.

Nussbaum, Martha C. 2018. "Minimum Core Obligations: Toward a Deeper Philosophical Inquiry." May 11. http://jamesgstewart.com/minimum-core-obligations-toward-a-deeper-philosophical-inquiry/.

Ohlin, Jens David. 2014. *The Assault on International Law*. New York: Oxford University Press.

Pavel, Carmen. 2015. *Divided Sovereignty: International Institutions and the Limits of State Authority*. 1st ed. Oxford: Oxford University Press.

Pavel, Carmen E., and David Lefkowitz. 2018. "Skeptical Challenges to International Law." *Philosophy Compass* 13 (8): 1–14.

Posner, Eric A. 2011. *The Perils of Global Legalism*. Reprint ed. Chicago: University of Chicago Press.

Ratner, Steven R. 2015. *The Thin Justice of International Law: A Moral Reckoning of the Law of Nations*. Oxford: Oxford University Press.

Rosen, Amanda M. 2015. "The Wrong Solution at the Right Time: The Failure of the Kyoto Protocol on Climate Change." *Politics & Policy* 43 (1): 30–58. https://doi.org/10.1111/polp.12105.

Rousseau, David L. 2002. "Motivations for Choice: The Salience of Relative Gains in International Politics." *Journal of Conflict Resolution* 46 (3): 394–426.

Rousseau, Jean-Jacques. 1987. *The Basic Political Writings*. 1st ed. Edited and translated by Donald A. Cress. Indianapolis, IN: Hackett Publishing.

Sabl, Andrew. 2012. *Hume's Politics: Coordination and Crisis in the "History of England"*. Princeton, NJ: Princeton University Press.

Shepsle, Kenneth. 1991. "Discretion, Institutions, and the Problem of Government Commitment." In *Social Theory for a Changing Society*, 1st ed., edited by Pierre Bourdieu and James S. Coleman, 245–63. Boulder, CO: Westview Press.

Sikkink, Kathryn. 2017. *Evidence for Hope: Making Human Rights Work in the 21st Century*. Princeton, NJ: Princeton University Press.

Stilz, Anna. 2011. *Liberal Loyalty: Freedom, Obligation, and the State*. Reprint. Princeton, NJ: Princeton University Press.

Tesón, Fernando R. 1998. *A Philosophy of International Law*. Boulder, CO: Westview Press.

Waldron, Jeremy. 1994. "John Locke: Social Contract Versus Political Anthropology." In *The Social Contract from Hobbes to Rawls*, edited by David Boucher and Paul Kelly, 51–72. London: Routledge.

Waltz, Kenneth. 1979. *Theory of International Politics*. 1st ed. New York: McGraw-Hill.

Weiler, J. H. H. 2003. "In Defense of the Status Quo, Europe's Constitutional Sonderweg." In *European Constitutionalism beyond the State*, edited by J. H. H. Weiler and Marlene Wind, 7–25. Cambridge, UK: Cambridge University Press.

Wenar, Leif. 2015. "Coercion in Cross-Border Property Rights." *Social Philosophy and Policy* 32 (1): 171–91.

Wenar, Leif. 2016. *Blood Oil: Tyrants, Violence, and the Rules That Run the World*. 1st ed. New York: Oxford University Press USA.

Williams, Howard. 1994. "Kant on the Social Contract." In *The Social Contract from Hobbes to Rawls*, edited by David Boucher and Paul Kelly, 135–48. London: Routledge.

1

Hume's Dynamic Coordination and International Law

Do individuals and states have reason to create and submit to the rules of international law? The tension between sovereign independence and international law is at the heart of recent initiatives by states to withdraw from the Paris Agreement or the International Criminal Court (*Guardian* 2017; Harrabin 2019). Yet one might think that states cannot have it both ways: they cannot reap the benefits of a system of international law that limits negative externalities from other states, restricts the use of violence, and ultimately guarantees a sphere of autonomous state action, and at the same time claim that international law is optional and their autonomy absolute. Just as individuals cannot benefit from domestic law while at the same time rejecting any interference with their freedom, so too states cannot be both restricted by international law and remain completely free to act according to the whims of their leaders or citizens. David Hume (1711–1776) offers a surprising resource for this argument, because he claims that the same reasons for adopting and developing a legal system at the domestic level also hold at the international level, even if the content and character of those rules will be different.

In this chapter I will explore and develop this Humean claim. Section XI of the *Treatise of Human Nature* offers great insights into the similarity and complementarity of domestic and international law (Hume 2000, 362–64).[1] Hume believes that the needs of individuals and states for

Law Beyond the State. Carmen E. Pavel, Oxford University Press (2021). © Oxford University Press.
DOI: 10.1093/oso/9780197543894.003.0002

social coordination are analogous: "The advantages, therefore, of peace, commerce, and mutual succour, make us extend to different kingdoms the same notions of justice, which take place among individuals" (Hume 2000, T 3.2.11.1). At the domestic level, Hume is famous for providing an account of dynamic coordination as the origin of law (Sabl 2012; Hardin 2007; McArthur 2004; Frazer 2012). I will show that the evolution of international customs and treaties offers an important study in Humean dynamic coordination.

This exploration takes place in the context of a skeptical take on the authority of existing international law and its further development. International law is said to be in turn inconsequential to state behavior, the product of irrational state action which goes against national interest in a world of anarchy, or detrimental to the project of democratic self-determination. Eric Posner's latest books aim to demonstrate the futility of international law when he says that "international law is [. . .] endogenous to state interests. It is not a check on state self-interest; it is a product of state self-interest" (Goldsmith and Posner 2005, 13). Due to the inherent inward-looking preferences of states, international law is incapable of creating order or solving collective action problems. Therefore we should maintain "a crisp analytic distinction between intrastate cooperation, which is capable of solving major nation-level collective action problems, and interstate cooperation, which is itself subject to collective action problems and thus cannot solve them, except in a very rudimentary fashion" (Posner 2011, 7). Posner is part of a new wave of legal scholars influenced by international relations realists who are skeptical that the world can be explained in terms of anything other than raw power. Offering a surprising combination of explanatory social science and normative analysis, realists such as Stephen Krasner say that "for realism, the central admonition for policy makers is that they must make prudent judgments. They must assess the consequences of their actions. They can never rely on moral precepts. Applying law and judicial proceedings to international relations reduces the likelihood of prudential calculations" (Krasner 2002, 267). This means in effect that states are better off ignoring the constraints of international law and can be considered to act irrationally when they take them seriously. But skepticism is not just the purview of realists. More recently, Martha Nussbaum claimed that international law is "leaching sovereignty away from the nation and its institutions, which are chosen by the nation's people, and turning it over to an international realm that is not decently accountable to people through their own political choices" (Nussbaum 2018). In Nussbaum's view, law can only be the product of a democratic community creating rules according to standards of accountably and inclusion which can only be obtained within states. To think that law beyond the state is possible and desirable is to imperil state-based projects of democratic self-governance. Other political philosophers and legal scholars have offered a more positive take on the authority and legitimacy of international law and its conformity with principles of justice (Tesón 1998; Buchanan 2004; Cohen 2012; Pavel 2015; Isiksel 2016; Criddle and Fox-Decent 2016; Ratner 2015). Still, these contributions take the existence of international law as a given, and many support it in this special sense of law where adherence to it is largely optional and consent revocable.

Drawing partly on David Hume's model of dynamic coordination, I will provide a moral justification for the necessity of developing international law into a legal system that has stronger law-like features. A reconstruction of Hume's account for international law explains how it can facilitate mutually beneficial cooperation internationally, by enhancing the pursuit of peace and of goals shared by various nations. Hume offers both an explanatory and a normative basis for this analysis. The explanatory basis traces the evolution of international law from customs responding to political communities' immediate interests for communicating and engaging with each other peacefully, to the complex treaties that characterize international law today, which speak to states' long-term self-interest and the interests of individuals through protections of their rights. The normative basis shows that gains made from stable, fair social norms which ensure the satisfaction of needs and interests are made possible by legal institutions that have rudimentary rule-of-law features. But there are limitations to Hume's account, stemming from his inattentiveness to the distinctive demands of recognizing individuals as sources of moral claims.

Thus, the rest of the chapter will provide, in the first part, an account of the tension between international law and state sovereignty, which is institutionalized in the requirement that the former's rules and institutions must be subject to express state consent. The second part will develop a Humean justification to support strengthening and expanding the authority of international law over states by focusing on the main functions of a legal system as Hume saw it. The third part describes the evolution of international law as broadly consistent with the Humean logic of dynamic coordination. The fourth shows why we need to supplement the Humean framework with a focus on the intrinsic and equal moral worth of individual human beings, in order to both give a fuller account of the norms of justice instantiated in international law and to explain the significant development of international human rights law. Despite his lacunae in this area, Hume remains helpful in illuminating why this particular area of international law continues to be weak.

In addition to reconstructing the Humean case for supporting the authority of international law, this chapter aims more generally to highlight the richness of Hume's understanding of law and political authority. It thus complements the valuable work produced in the last few decades, which recovers his neglected insights on the nature of political authority, justice, game theory, and law (Sabl 2012; Hanley 2011; Sagar 2018; Frazer 2012; Krause 2004; Hardin 2007; McArthur 2004; Postema 1988).

INTERNATIONAL LAW AND STATE CONSENT

International law continues to be suspended between the internal logic of law, which requires a system of uniformly binding rules, and the internal logic of sovereignty, which requires that states are recognized and entrenched as political entities that make their own rules free from interference from the outside (Hart 2012, 213–37). International law has some distinct, unusual features for a legal system. One of its most important sources, treaty law, is consensual, in the sense that its rules only bind states when they have explicitly agreed to it. Even when states consent to a treaty, they can register reservations to some of its provisions, which subsequently become nonbinding.[2] Some states consider authoritative the interpretation of their international obligations provided by their own national courts, even when their interpretation conflicts with that provided by international courts.[3] The various international courts and dispute resolution mechanisms such as the International Court of Justice and the International Criminal Court lack compulsory jurisdiction (except in the case of Security Council referral), which makes it easy for states to extricate themselves from accountability when they violate international rules.[4] Jus cogens norms, obligations erga omnes, customary law, and the decisions of the Security Council bind states without their consent, but states manage to extricate themselves even from these binding norms and institutions (Cassese 2012; McGregor 2006).[5]

State consent is the cornerstone of international law. The VCLT clearly states in Article 34: "A treaty does not create either obligations or rights for a third State without its consent."[6] Each country's foundational legal rules determine when and under what conditions adherence to international law is possible or desirable. In the United States, for instance, recent constitutional practice has cemented the idea that that only constitutionally authorized domestic bodies, such as the president, the legislature, and the Supreme Court, can decide when to adopt an international treaty, and what its consequences for domestic law are (Paulsen 2009; Hathaway, McElroy, and Solow 2012; Verdirame 2007). One might think that this is an unusual position, reflective of the fact that the United States has the power to situate itself outside of major international treaties with fewer costs and to see such treaties as damaging its national interest, but in fact this position of constitutional supremacy is quite common. "Monist" states such as France and Netherlands do grant automatic authority to international law without the need for implementing legislation, but importantly, only to the treaties they explicitly consent to.[7]

This leaves plenty of room for both weak and powerful countries to withhold consent to treaties solving collective action problems such as climate change, or to give consent to rules and withhold consent to institutions tasked with interpreting and applying the rules, such as international courts. This latter feature of international law renders it less costly for states to breach international rules. International law is thus in a rather unique position of binding its subjects (mostly states) only when they agree to its authority, and only in the manner in which the subjects deem appropriate. This is a rather weak form of law, if we can call it law at all. Increasingly, customary law and other nonoptional norms such as jus cogens create obligations for states without their consent, but states continue to guard their sovereignty jealously in the face of these developments.

Why should this matter? At the heart of the question about the proper relationship of national and international law is the more general question of the nature and the purpose of law. Can law be such that adherence to rules is optional, the interpretation is left to the law's subjects, and the subjects can decide unilaterally they are no longer bound by some or all of the rules? How to best understand the authority of independent states to make rules for their own territories: absolute, or subject to some constrains set by international law? Can international law determine the rights individuals have against their own governments or the governments of other states? Can states be restrained by rules that regulate their interactions with each other? These questions about the nature of law and international law more specifically are questions about the extent and authority of state power and therefore foundational questions of political philosophy. Taking inspiration from Hume, I will argue that the reasons to defend the establishment of laws and legal institutions inside political communities are the same as the reasons to establish it across political communities. If one believes there is a general justification for law, that justification applies to international law as well.

HUME ON INTERNATIONAL LAW

Hume emerges as an unlikely figure to argue for a justification for domestic and international law based on common principles. He thought that law draws its origin from group conflict: "And so far am I from thinking with some philosophers, that men are utterly incapable of society without government, that I assert the first rudiments of government to arise from quarrels, not among men of the same society, *but among those of different societies* (emphasis added)" (Hume 2000, T 3.2.8.1). Conflict creates the necessity of establishing rules of mutual forbearance, and only once those are instituted, the possibility of cooperation emerges. Hume explains further that

> the three fundamental rules of justice, the stability of possession, its transference by consent, and the performance of promises, are duties of princes, as well as of subjects. The same interest produces the same effect in both cases. Where possession has no stability, there must be perpetual war. Where property is not transferr'd by consent, there can be no commerce. Where promises are not observ'd, there can be no leagues nor alliances. The advantages, therefore, of peace, commerce, and mutual succour, make us extend to different kingdoms the same notions of justice, which take place among individuals. (Hume 2000, T3.2.11.2)

The three fundamental rules of justice, namely the stability of possessions or territories in the case of states, their peaceful transfer, and respecting promises, create the demand for international rules just as they create the demand for domestic rules. In their absence, war is likely to persist, and the possibility of stable cooperation and growth diminishes or disappears.

Hume was not alone in drawing parallels between the dynamic of interaction among individuals and that of states. As Richard Tuck shows, this was a leitmotif of natural law theorists, who searched for the principles of right conduct to govern individuals and nations discoverable by reason. Hugo Grotius, for example, claimed there is no remarkable difference between individuals and states, and for him and Thomas Hobbes, "self-preservation was a paramount principle" of both (Tuck 2001, 5, 82, 85, 129; Grotius 2017; Hobbes 1994). Peace was the necessary corollary of self-preservation as a right of both individuals and states, and the way to achieve peace was to follow natural law precepts as an account of universal morality.

Grotius made much of the parallel between individuals and states and the natural law rules which apply to both. In his seminal works *Mare Liberum* and *De Jure Belli ac Pacis* he argued that the law of nature directs states, just as much as individuals, to reconcile self-preservation with social life (Grotius 2004, 2005). The rights of states derive from those of individuals, and Grotius was able to derive a number of principles which should govern the relations among states, such as sovereign independence, mutual toleration, peaceful commercial relations, humanitarian intervention, and the principle of the freedom of the seas, all of which have exercised an indisputable influence on the development of international law since (Tuck 2001; Blom 2019). Grotius relied on natural law principles as the basis of a proto-contractarian system of rules meant to bind states in their interactions with one another.

Hobbes, like Grotius, saw the analogy between the natural condition of men and the international order, but drew a different conclusion, namely that international law is not possible: states have a right to self-preservation just as individuals do, but in the absence of a state to preside over all states, a global leviathan, states cannot overcome the dynamics of perpetual conflict of the state of nature in international politics. More importantly, he saw binding rules on states as incompatible with principles of absolute sovereignty (Hobbes 1994, 78, 110–18). There is not, and there cannot be, a global social contract to create international law. In the anarchy of international politics, only natural law principles apply, and they do so weakly, just as they do among individuals in the state of nature. Inspired by both Grotius and Hobbes, it was Immanuel Kant who provided the most ambitious proposal for international cooperation, in the form of a confederation of free states, but the rules envisioned as the foundation of this confederation were limited to the preservation of peace and the creation of the conditions of universal hospitality (Kant 1983).

Hume notoriously rejected both the social contract and natural law as explanatory and normative frameworks for law and social cooperation. He claimed that social cooperation can exist without government, and that we cannot understand what rules people develop by studying their nature in the abstract (Hume 2000, T.3.2.8.1; Buckle and Castiglione 1991).

On Hume's view, neither rules not their interpretation rest on a realm of objective, shared principles waiting to be discovered and applied. Instead, rules come about in a contingent and somewhat arbitrary fashion, and they depend on patterns of human interaction which give rise to them. Hume proposes a very different picture of human sociability, one that I will argue provides a better empirical and explanatory account of the evolution of international law and of its limitations from the standpoint of justice. Hume's alternative account of the evolution of social rules, including law, is that they develop gradually, through a process of dynamic coordination, which allows individuals to develop common interests even when they are initially stuck in conflict (Buckle and Castiglione 1991).

Hume departed significantly from the idea of morality discoverable by reason alone, a feature common to natural law theories. Reason is limited when solutions to one coordination problem are many; they emerge somewhat arbitrarily and grow in a path-dependent manner out of previous conventions to provide answers to new problems (Sabl 2012, 27). But Hume agreed with natural law theorists that conventions will not be completely arbitrary; they will follow a logic internal to the nature of humans as beings with certain needs, interests, and proclivities, such as the inclination to favor one's own self-preservation and interests, but also to sympathetically engage the interests and needs of other fellow humans. And these features are common to the evolution of international law (Hume 2000, T3.2.1.19).

If we take seriously Hume's claim that the problems of cooperation are similar among individuals and states, we need to ask whether a general justification for law among individuals can transfer to international law. One of the justifications which transfers easily is that law often originates out of conflict, which is a condition between individuals as well as states: "and indeed this assertion is so far just, that different nations, as well as private persons, require mutual assistance; at the same time that their selfishness and ambition are perpetual sources of war and discord" (Hume 2000, T 3.2.11.1). Similar to Hume, for the first scholars of international law the pervasiveness of war served as the rationale for a system of international rules. The Spanish scholastics Francisco de Vitoria and

Francisco Suarez sought to discover general principles for regulating the use of violence (Lorca 2012, 1086–90; Vitoria 1991; Beneyto and Varela 2017; Scott and Butler 2014). Hugo Grotius and Samuel Pufendorf, both of whom exercised perhaps the most lasting influence on international law, count among their main contributions works on the law of war and peace (Lorca 2012, 1098–1105; Tuck 2001; Grotius 2017; Barbeyrac, Pufendorf, and Percivale 2011).

This preoccupation with war reflected the times these thinkers lived in. War between monarchical powers was a regular means of solving disagreements; the human and economic costs were catastrophic and erased the gains made by stable, developed internal legal systems. While these early theorists of international law provided general rules and principles for regulating war, they talked much less about the problem John Locke identified, namely how to restrict the partiality of legal subjects, in this case states (Locke 1988, 275, 281). Having international rules to regulate the conduct of war is not sufficient if states are left to interpret those rules themselves. Indeed, Grotius's insistence that sovereign states ought to be trusted to interpret the indeterminate clauses of their contracts on their own, because their sense of justice and universal right will lead them to converge on their interpretations or at least to remain restrained in judging how far their authority extends, should strike us as naïve (Grotius 2005, II.XVI). It is a lacuna in theorizing about the necessity of international law, both in the writings of these earlier thinkers and more recently, that there is so little emphasis on common, authoritative institutions for the settlement of legal disputes and the interpretation of the common rules of behavior.

War was not just a problem for European monarchical states. R. P. Anand, a scholar prominent in Third World approaches to international law, criticized the Eurocentrism of the narratives that led to the creation of international law. He argued that law grows slowly to fulfill the needs of people locally and "the needs of men organized in separate communities" internationally (Lorca 2012, 1042). International law responds to a universal need for stability and predictability. Rules for governing the interaction of different political communities do not have an exclusive European pedigree. In some form or other, rules for regulating war, the exchange of diplomatic representatives, the treatment of foreigners, and the regulation of trade were present in ancient civilizations around the world, from China to India, Egypt, Islamic states, the Roman Empire, and premodern Europe. These insights are recovered by new histories of international law that aim to move beyond the Eurocentrism of earlier approaches (Fassbender et al. 2012).

But if Hume rejected natural law and the social contract, what did he leave in their place to account for the origin and moral authority of law? Hume's most important contribution to political philosophy is arguably his account of dynamic coordination, namely the idea that we learn how to live peacefully with other people by adjusting our behavior to theirs (Hume 2000, 307–64; Sabl 2012, 6). His story of the evolution of law offers a unique framework for understanding the evolution of international law as well. Hume thought human beings first develop formal and informal social conventions which prescribe rules for how they should interact in small communities. The recognition of the role of property rules for social peace was fundamental for Hume. People come to gradually recognize the importance of reciprocal respect for other people's property: "[T]he rule concerning the stability of possession [is] deriv'd from human conventions, it arises gradually, and acquires force by a slow progression, and by our repeated experience of the inconveniences of transgressing it" (Hume 2000, T 3.2.2.10). Rules such as respect for possessions are shaped by evolving common interests into what Hume calls conventions.

At first these conventions are sustained by mutual sympathy and reciprocity among kin. Conventions in small communities can create a sense of order but do not take us very far. We still inhabit a state that Michael Frazer describes as "lawless clannishness," where we can be secure inside our communities but find ourselves constantly under threat from the outside (Frazer 2012, 69–70). We trade war for peace by extending prevailing conventions or negotiating new ones among an increasing number of people, who are now part of an enlarged circle of mutual sympathy and reciprocity. The conventions themselves deepen and become more stable and law-like, as both the original participants and the new ones can grasp the long-term benefits of social coordination through rules (Frazer 2012, 70–71).

Importantly, these conventions which engender peace and cooperation precede government. Thus, Hume offered a rival account of politics, and ultimately of law, to that of Hobbes, based on human sociability, which precedes government and guarantees the foundation for it (Sagar 2018, 11–12, 54–66). Conventions precede government, and as they multiply and change dynamically to include greater numbers of people and answers to new problems of social cooperation, we also enlarge our sympathy toward others. Once social practices are established, we expect other people to comply with them, and we develop a sense of approbation and disapprobation for actions that fall outside of those practices and are injurious to those in the enlarged circle (Sayre-McCord 2013; Frazer 2012, 73–75). Conventions grow independently of our moral approbation or disapprobation but help cultivate it. They instill the habits of mind and virtues that make it possible for us to consider the interests of increasing numbers of individuals (Frazer 2012, 78; Sabl 2012, 49–50). Against natural law theorists, Hume argues that our sense of justice is itself developed by conventions and does not come from unsocialized reflection: "that those impressions, which give rise to this sense of justice, are not natural to the mind of man, but arise from artifice and human conventions" (Hume 2000, T 3.2.2.21). Justice is itself a kind of convention: "[T]hus justice establishes itself by a kind of convention or agreement; that is, by a sense of interest, suppos'd to be common to all, and where every single act is perform'd in expectation that others are to perform the like" (Hume 2000, T 3.2.2.22). Justice for Hume consists not only in doing what is right in some abstruse, abstract sense. What is right is determined by other people's actions and expectations, and mutual reliance on their ability to follow rules makes cooperation possible.

Social conventions evolve from small communities to larger ones, and both individual and social learning takes place. Individuals come to reconsider their self-interest in a way that incorporates to a growing extent the interests of others. Communities sometimes accidentally, sometimes deliberately, stumble upon solutions to a wide range of coordination and cooperation problems, such as language, traffic rules, units of measurements, money, rules for property, and contracts. Self-interest plays a key role in creating and maintaining those rules. Yet according to Hume, self-interest makes rules vulnerable as well, due to the fact that people will often prefer a trivial advantage they can obtain by breaking them to the observance of justice that they make possible. But social co-operation also teaches us that others who follow the law reap long-term benefits, and they serve as a model for us to refrain from pursuing short-sighted self-interest. Hume says:

> This is the reason why men so often act in contradiction to their known interest; and in particular why they prefer any trivial advantage, that is present, to the maintenance of order in society, which so much depends on the observance of justice. The consequences of every breach of equity seem to lie very remote, and are not able to counter-ballance any immediate advantage, that may be reap'd from it. Your example both pushes me forward in this way by imitation, and also affords me a new reason for any breach of equity, by shewing me, that I should be the cully of my integrity, if I alone shou'd impose on myself a severe restraint amidst the licentiousness of others. (Hume 2000, T 3.2.7.3)

Learning about the benefits of social cooperation enables us to reflectively correct our sense of self-interest as we develop an interest in co-operation itself (Frazer 2012, 71). Thus, while Posner may be right that international law springs from the self-interest of states, just as law more generally springs from the self-interest of individuals, it does not follow that it cannot act as a constraint. Legal subjects, when appropriately socialized, develop an interest in maintaining the rules quite irrespective of the latter's effect on their immediate self-interest, and in developing the attitudes and institutions to reinforce the rules against nonconforming others.

While law precedes government, legal conventions are made more effective, and their benefits extended to all, by institutionalized systems of rules, namely by laws made by governments, aided by their impartial application by magistrates (Hume 2000, T 3.2.7.7). They provide additional reasons for individuals, either via uniform sanctions or simply due to the widespread obedience that political authority inspires, to restrain their natural partiality and to refrain from pursuing shortsighted self-interest at the expense of their long-term interest and the common good. In addition, general conventions also facilitate common projects and growth. Two neighbors can build a dam together, but hundreds or thousands of individuals face severe collective action problems in the absence of general rules (Hume 2000, T 3.2.7.8). Communities contain people of complementary skills who can cooperate and create more and better together. And it is the internal security of the society that makes it all possible (Hume 2000, T 3.2.2.3).

Conventions of authority are crucial in Hume's view for stability and peace. Andrew Sabl explains persuasively the reason for their prominence in Hume's thinking. Conventions of authority are conventions about how power changes hands, who is entitled to exercise it, based on which rules, and what are the limits of that power. They facilitate peaceful transition from one ruler to the next and orderly, incremental changes in the rules themselves. They protect us from "the risk of civil war on the one hand and the excesses of arbitrary power on the other" (Sabl 2012, 33). To mediate political compromises, conventions of authority must precede them temporarily and thus rest outside the normal space of politics (Sabl 2012, 15, 21, 29, 32–33, 90–156; Hardin 2007). Therefore, we get an account of political authority and law that offers a compelling alternative to Hobbes. But conventions of authority tend to acquire their legitimacy only after they have proven successful at mediating political compromise, even if their origins predate the compromises they solve.[8] Conventions of authority must be especially stable since they serve the most basic ends of security and peace (Sabl 2012, 32; Sagar 2018, 123–29).

If conventions of authority are essential, so are the substantive and formal characteristics of the law. Law's main purpose is to create the regularity that helps us orient ourselves to others, plan for the future, and reap the fruits of our plans. Property and contracts are the result of uniform, binding conventions that maintain stability of possessions and the performance of promises (Morris and Brown 2016). Therefore, laws related to property and contracts are fundamental to any legal system, and Hume equates their observance with justice.

In addition to substantive requirements, a legal system must meet some formal requirements as well. The formal requirements take the form of rule-of-law features. Hume says that the extensive benefits of social cooperation are better achieved by generally applicable laws, which are stable in time and across circumstances and are independent of social class (McArthur 2004, 153). They are rigid, in the sense that they do not make too much room for the discretionary judgment of the magistrate (McArthur 2004, 154). They are applied impartially and uniformly, including to those who make and apply law (McArthur 2004, 161–62). They are public. Punishing people for breaking secret laws is revenge, not justice. Only law constrained by the rule of law can perform its function of preventing conflict and protecting the interests of the participants in social cooperation (McArthur 2004, 155).

It is this account of dynamic coordination, coupled with the insights in Section XI of the *Treatise of Human Nature*, which offers a distinctive Humean account of the similarity and the complementarity of domestic and international law (Hume 2000, 362–64). Hume believes that the needs of individual persons and states for social coordination are analogous:

> When men have found by experience, that 'tis impossible to subsist without society, and that 'tis impossible to maintain society, while they give free course to their appetites; so urgent an interest quickly restrains their actions, and imposes an obligation to observe those rules, which we call *the laws of justice*. [. . .] The same *natural* obligation of interest takes place among independent kingdoms, and gives rise to the same *morality*; so that no one of ever so corrupt morals will approve of a prince, who voluntarily, and of his own accord, breaks his word, or violates any treaty. (Hume 2000, T 3.2.11.4)

The interaction of individuals and kingdoms follows the same logic. They share the same interests and, as a result, the same morality. It is unjust for a person to break her promises just as it is for a prince. And it is unjust of a state to usurp another's territory just as it is for individuals. Therefore, they will share the same general principles to regulate their conduct.

Yet Hume sees differences, too. He believes that those differences mean that individuals and nations will regulate themselves by different rules, although aiming at the same general principles (Hume 2000, T 3.2.11.1). The difference does not consist only in the different substance of the rules, but also in the different force with which they apply: "[T]ho' the morality of princes has the same *extent*, yet it has not the same *force* as that of private persons, and may lawfully be transgress'd from a more trivial motive" (Hume 2000, T 3.2.11.3). What could possibly be the basis of the assertion that states can break their agreements more easily? The answer is to be found in the different degrees of necessity domestic and international law respond to:

> But here we may observe, that tho' the intercourse of different states be advantageous, and even sometimes necessary, yet it is not so necessary nor advantageous as that among individuals, without which 'tis utterly impossible for human nature ever to subsist. Since, therefore, the *natural* obligation to justice, among different states, is not so strong as among individuals, the *moral* obligation, which arises from it, must partake of its weakness; and we must necessarily give a greater indulgence to a prince or minister, who deceives another; than to a private gentleman, who breaks his word of honour. (Hume 2000, T 3.2.11.4)

In other words, Hume does not believe that states breaking their promises to each other will have the same devastating consequences as individuals doing the same. He is in one sense correct. Once we have a certain level of domestic stability through laws which are widely respected, the consequences of breaking a promise to some distant and little-known prince may be low. But in another way, Hume seriously underestimates the extent to which international peace and stability and the rules respecting the territorial integrity of states operate as preconditions of peace in domestic legal systems. In the case of constant war with neighboring countries, the gains in stability and prosperity made by one's legal system are likely to stagnate and even to reverse over time.

Hume repeats the opposite view. In a passage in the essay *The Enquiry Concerning the Principles of Morals*, he says: "[H]ere is the difference between kingdoms and individuals. Human nature cannot, by any means, subsist, without the association of individuals; and that association never could have place, were no regard paid to the laws of equity and justice. . . . But nations can subsist without intercourse" (Hume 2006, 213). Yet Hume is wrong to say that nations can subsist without intercourse. He may be right that at different historical times communities could have subsisted without relying on each other much for economic resources, but that time of minimal subsistence and economic autarchy has long passed.[9] A different interpretation of Hume is that he is simply making a conceptual point. Human sociability is inconceivable without law, while states are conceivable without international law. Although we can grant this conceptual point, we must resist taking it too far. Hume is simply incorrect if we take on board the current reality of intense interaction among separate political communities, in which states need to create rules in order to resolve territorial disputes, solve collective action problems such as climate change, divide air transport routes, etc. The large numbers of countries in existence today routinely cooperate over the division of border resources such as waterways, the management of negative externalities they inflict on each other, and the necessity of regular diplomatic relations, all of which require rule-based interaction.

One might even argue that the failures of such rules, which lead to war, conflict over borders and resources, and the inability to solve problems such as global warming, are just as large threats to human survival or even greater than threats to the association of individuals in well-regulated political communities. Some of these threats, like the possibility of destruction brought about by nuclear technology or climate change, are new, and Hume could not have possibly anticipated them. But he did understand that conventions arise in response to contingent and unpredictable forces which shape how human beings interact, and the importance of international rules is more acute now than it was in Hume's time. Therefore, Hume is overstating the disanalogy, and acknowledging this shortcoming in Hume's thought enables us to give a stronger rather than weaker justification for developing a system of international law. Although Hume lacked some clarity in his account of the necessity of developing a system of international law, he provides a sound basis on which to reconstruct a case for international law that is as strong as, if not stronger than, the case for domestic law.

Hume's account of dynamic coordination will help us see, in the next section, why Hobbes's skepticism about the possibility of a system of international law is not compelling. Hobbes thought law is not possible without a government to coordinate individual action and enforce the rules.[10] But Hume established the possibility of law without government via the evolution of conventions among small-scale communities, and a similar evolution can be observed via customs and treaties in international law in the absence of a global Leviathan.

A HUMEAN MODEL OF DYNAMIC COORDINATION IN INTERNATIONAL LAW

I have made the case that Hume's account of dynamic coordination gives us a different and much richer perspective on the necessity of developing a robust system of rules at the international level, one which matches more closely the evolution of international law and enables us both to observe the limitations of this evolution as well as understand its possibilities. Indeed, the point of this section is to show precisely why the Humean account of dynamic coordination can explain the slow evolution of international law from customary law to the complex formal treaties and institutional arrangements we see today, which a contractualist, natural law–inspired view cannot. The division of air traffic routes or the creation of nuclear nonproliferation treaties relies on technologies which could hardly be anticipated during the heyday of modern social contract theories and which create challenges for interstate interactions with their own demands for regulation.

International law's genealogy offers a study in dynamic coordination. Dynamic coordination explains the incremental, unpredictable, and contingent development of international conventions from custom to formal treaties and institutions tasked with their interpretation and application. Customary international norms allowed states to coordinate expectations in areas essential to their interactions, such as the exchanging of ambassadors, the treatment of each other's citizens, and the regulation of trade. Hume already saw the fruits of that coordination and observed that what we call "the laws of nations" comprise "the sacredness of the persons of ambassadors, the declaration of war, the abstaining from poison'd arms, with other duties of that kind, which are evidently calculated for the commerce, that is peculiar to different societies" (Hume 2000, T 3.2.11.1). Customary norms have created the predictability and stability countries required in the absence of formal treaties, evolving from bilateral agreements to the sophisticated legal rules we see operating in international law today.

International law has moved more decisively past the lawless clannishness of Hume's basic conventions with the creation of formal multilateral treaties. Today it contains treaties whose role is precisely to balance conflicting interests and assign rights of way among multiple states, so that disagreements are anticipated and resolved and large-scale cooperation is made possible. The law of the sea offers a great example of law-like cooperation. States with commercial fleets have sought wide access to international waters, while coastal states have wanted to restrict such access along their shores. And various states have demanded access to the exploitation of the same ocean resources. First through a series of customary norms, and more recently through the United Nations Convention on the Law of the Sea (UNCLOS; 1982), the law of the sea regime now regulates, among other things, control over coastal waters, the allocation of fishing rights, pollution, criminal jurisdiction, seabed mining, marine scientific research, and passage through straits for shipping and military vessels.

Hume's account of dynamic cooperation is based on an evolved sense of self-interest. The coordination function of law is accomplished by treaties that serve the states' immediate and converging interests (Guzman 2010, 25–48). States can coordinate easily in situations in which they prefer to create a mutually binding rule, but may have different views about which rule is the best. A good example of a solution to a coordination problem is the treaty creating the 1865 International Telegraphic Union, by which states agreed on the type of equipment and the language used to transmit telegraphic messages. Once the treaty helps states coordinate on a language and other rules for communicating, they have strong incentives to comply because they have little to gain by defecting. The treaty selects rules as equilibrium points, and the more states join the treaty, the more it becomes the dominant equilibrium. Countless treaties like this have been signed since the mid-nineteenth century, but they fade from view because they run smoothly, compliance rates are extremely high, and there is little incentive to cheat. A modern-day example is international conventions that regulate aircraft travel and airspace routes. The Convention on International Civil Aviation (1944), also known as the Chicago Convention, is a foundational document, amended repeatedly in light of advances in technology and learning about what rules work best.[11]

However, states find themselves in a variety of situations in which their short-term interests and their enlightened, long-term interests may be at odds. In these contexts, states have incentives to both create rules and defect from them, and these incentives interact in complex ways. This is why tremendous progress in certain areas of international law, such as the protection of environmental resources, human rights, war making, and economic law, coexists with significant violations of the rules by states. Because it is still a primitive legal system in many respects, one can see the operation of shortsighted self-interest in the often-hypocritical insistence of states like the United States, Russia, and China that other states should follow international law, but that its rules do not necessarily apply to them. Or in the unwillingness to create strong enforcement mechanisms for binding rules for fear that their sovereign authority will be curtailed. Or in the many states' unwillingness to join or make effective human rights treaties, or the International Criminal Court, for fear that their own citizens or officials will be targeted for prosecution.

Perhaps the most difficult area for international cooperation is human rights protection. Although treaties in this area have proliferated, states gain little by complying, and treaties often tie the hands of the political elites, for whom joining such treaties is costly. Still, strong, authoritative law can transform the incentives of states to cooperate in the process of having states deliberate about the appropriate rules (Bicchieri and Muldoon 2014). The lawmaking process itself increases incentives for compliance and cooperation by transforming the identities and interests of states themselves and by creating conventions of authority that facilitate the adoption of pro-legal attitudes in the law's subjects. International legal rules also decrease incentives for defection due to sanctions that raise the cost of noncompliance, and in no small measure due to mechanisms such as reputation, reciprocity, and retaliation (Guzman 2010, 33–48).

Hume anticipated one of the main challenges of international law today: to persuade states to forgo shortsighted self-interest and adopt a more consistent commitment to international rules, for the sake of the long-term benefits of an international legal order for all. States like the United States struggle with the conflicting impulse of short-term flouting of the rules and the insistence that it is in everyone's interest to follow them in the long term. Its dismissal of the *Avena* judgment of the International Court of Justice in *Sanchez Llama v. Oregon* is a symptom of the former. Its insistence that China follow the decision of the Permanent Court of Arbitration in the South China Sea dispute, which found China in violation of the UNCLOS, is an example of the latter (Brunnstrom and Spetalnick 2016).

Hume helps us both understand and defend the subsequent dramatic development of international law. He defended substantive rules at the international level to ensure the stability of possessions, their transfer by consent, and the keeping of promises. Respecting these conventions is a key mechanism whereby nations have managed to avert constant war, even if war inevitably breaks out at times. While Hume does not explicitly defend international decision-making bodies (they did not exist during his time), his theory gives us reasons to understand their value. This evolutionary account enables us to identify important constitutive moments in the development of international law as we see it today, from customary rules regarding the exchange of diplomatic representatives, to formal agreements as treaties which create dense networks of institutions of adjudication and enforcement, such as the UN Charter or the WTO.

The lesson we must draw from Hume is not just that rules are needed to address problems of cooperation among states which have a similar structure to problems of cooperation among individuals. It is rather that rules governing relations among states become effective when they are institutionalized, benefit from stable conventions of authority, are applied generally and impartially, and are interpreted by courts insulated from political persuasion. To conclude, for Hume, as well as for early scholars of international law, the problems of cooperation among individuals and cooperation among states are similar, and law is meant to provide solutions for both. This insight is worth recovering in support of the further strengthening of international law toward a system with stronger law-like features.

THE LIMITS OF THE HUMEAN ACCOUNT

It is important to note, however, that there are important limitations to Hume's account of justice at the domestic level, and this will be reflected in limitations of a possible reconstruction of his argument in support of international law. The main problem with Hume's account of justice is that it is too narrow, consisting mostly of rules regarding property and contracts. A proper account of justice goes beyond the Humean one, to include affirming the value of individuals as sources of moral claims.[12] Law performs a unique social function by rectifying wrongs done to individuals, by making sure people are given their due and treated with dignity as sources of moral claims. And law must fulfill this function partly (though not wholly) independent of the consequences for peace, property, and social cooperation. Social norms that evolve and spread informally, and norms of personal morality about what individual people think is right or wrong, could go some way toward correcting injustice, but laws ensure general and impartial standards about the appropriate ways of treating fellow human beings.

The "dignity protecting" function of law has a more convoluted relationship to self-interest. Self-interest properly understood plays a key role in creating and maintaining legal rules. Individuals engage in the process of creating legal rules because they can reap long-term benefits from peace, stability, and extended social cooperation. But human rights protection is different. Individuals and groups in a privileged position to make the law often benefit from harming and oppressing vulnerable individuals and minorities, and social peace may rest on the oppressed not pressing their demands for proper treatment. While the conflict-preventing and coordinating functions of law are mostly a reaction to self-regarding reasons, the rights-promoting function of law requires more than self-interest. It requires other-regarding reasons, namely to regard other individuals as having moral worth and as being sources of moral claims on us.

Human rights theorists talk about rights as norms that help to protect all people everywhere from severe political, legal, and social abuses (Tasioulas 2013; Cruft, Liao, and Renzo 2015, 217–360; Beitz 2009; Nickel 2007; Griffin 2009). These norms are made effective when they are incorporated in the actual legal systems of national and international law. International human rights law defines states' responsibilities to their own citizens and acts as a surrogate when states are unable to protect the rights of their citizens or are themselves the primary violators. Situations of failed states, refugees, and stateless individuals are additional, distinctive concerns of international law.

If Hume is right about the evolution of the law, historically speaking, we would expect this function of law to become entrenched last in developed legal systems. Hume was not directly concerned with the protection of vulnerable individuals and minorities, and this protection cannot be explained solely in terms of coordination or cooperation. But Hume was right that the coordinative function of law typically gets off the ground first, because it speaks directly to the self-interest of the most powerful agents in society. The protection of the weak and vulnerable is adopted after law as a system of social coordination acquires social legitimacy. Only subsequently is the rule of law used in the service of protecting rights impartially and of making sure the lawmaking and law-applying institutions are limited in their exercise of power.

The commitment to the minimal demands of justice has been the slowest and costliest victory in domestic law, and it went hand in hand with strengthening of the rule of law, the idea that rules must be applied impartially to all, including political officials or powerful elites; that they must be publicized; that they must be clear, stable, and just; and that the process by which laws are enacted, administered, and enforced is accessible, fair, and efficient.

Massive state failures regarding states' protection of their citizens' basic rights leave scope for international law to cover large gaps in governance. International law ensures an additional basis, however minimal, for rights protection for those individuals who fall outside of the scope of government protection, either because their county's legal system explicitly excludes them or because their county's legal system collapses, as in the case of failed states. Jus cogens norms are norms that protect individuals against some of the most serious violations of their rights and are a good starting point for inserting a minimal standard of justice into the international legal system (Criddle and Fox-Decent 2009). The creation of the International Criminal Court is a step in that direction.

As Steven Ratner persuasively shows, international law already conforms to a "thin" notion of justice, by having rules that respect, in the sense that they do not interfere with, basic rights (2015, 64–100). The norms of sovereign equality, noninterference in the affairs of other states, and the ban on the use of force are important to an understanding of justice as rights protection at the international level. Absent such norms, we would see even more trampling on individual and group rights and the undermining of the peace that makes such rights protection possible (Ratner 2015, 103–42). Timidly, international law attempts to incorporate a more substantive notion of justice by adopting more demanding obligations for states to protect, promote, and enforce their citizens' rights and by creating international institutions with the jurisdiction to adjudicate claims about noncompliance. But it remains the case that many of these obligations are weak and only apply to states on a quasi-consensual basis, that is to states which voluntarily undertake obligations associated with human rights treaties, unless the Security Council intervenes.

CONCLUSION

Drawing on Hume, I have argued that there is a general justification for developing international law into an authoritative, nonoptional system of rules, and this justification shares many features in common with justifications for domestic law. If such justification is available, states should be willing to create rules and institutions of international law with greater force and authority than they are willing to do now. At the very least, international law should contain rules regulating the use of violence, the protection of states' territory and resources, minimal benchmarks for individual rights, and compulsory jurisdiction for courts to interpret these rules and adjudicate disagreements arising out of their implementation by states.

Besides giving us a fuller measure of the richness and applicability of Hume's conception of law, the general lesson of this reconstruction of Hume's account of the necessity of international law is the following. Making international law more law-like does not entail reproducing all or even most of the features of effective domestic legal systems. But it does entail reproducing the minimal features that enable its subjects to reap the benefits of peaceful cooperation, such as some obligatory rules that apply to all, regardless of choice: restrictions on the free use of violence, courts with compulsory jurisdiction, and rights protections for individuals and states. These features enable states to adjust their behavior to the actions of others, plan for the future, engage in cooperative activities, and solve collective action and public goods problems.

REFERENCES

Avena and Other Mexican Nationals, Mexico v United States, ICGJ 8 (ICJ 2004).

Barbeyrac, Jean, Samuel Pufendorf, and William Percivale. 2011. *Of the Law of Nature and Nations*. Charleston: Nabu Press.

Beitz, Charles R. 2009. *The Idea of Human Rights*. New York: Oxford University Press.

Beneyto, José María, and Justo Corti Varela, eds. 2017. *At the Origins of Modernity: Francisco de Vitoria and the Discovery of International Law*. New York: Springer.

Bicchieri, Cristina, and Ryan Muldoon. 2014. "Social Norms." In *Stanford Encyclopedia of Philosophy*, edited by Edward N. Zalta, Spring ed. http://plato.stanford.edu/archives/spr2014/entries/social-norms/.

Blom, Andrew. 2019. "Grotius, Hugo." In *Internet Encyclopedia of Philosophy*. Accessed December 2, 2019. https://www.iep.utm.edu/grotius/#H3.

Brunnstrom, David, and Matt Spetalnick. 2016. "U.S. Warns China against Provocations Once Court Rules on Sea Claims." Reuters, June 22. http://www.reuters.com/article/us-southchinasea-usa-china-idUSKCN0Z82RD.

Buchanan, Allen. 2004. *Justice, Legitimacy, and Self-Determination: Moral Foundations for International Law*. New York: Oxford University Press.

Buckle, Stephen, and Dario Castiglione. 1991. "Hume's Critique of the Contract Theory." *History of Political Thought* 12 (3): 457–80.

Cassese, Antonio, ed. 2012. *Realizing Utopia: The Future of International Law*. Oxford: Oxford University Press.

Cohen, Jean L. 2012. *Globalization and Sovereignty: Rethinking Legality, Legitimacy, and Constitutionalism*. Cambridge, UK: Cambridge University Press.

Criddle, Evan J., and Evan Fox-Decent. 2009. "A Fiduciary Theory of Jus Cogens." *Yale Journal of International Law* 34: 331–87.

Criddle, Evan J., and Evan Fox-Decent. 2016. *Fiduciaries of Humanity: How International Law Constitutes Authority*. New York: Oxford University Press.

Cruft, Rowan, S. Matthew Liao, and Massimo Renzo, eds. 2015. *Philosophical Foundations of Human Rights*. Oxford: Oxford University Press.

Dyzenhaus, David. 2014. "Hobbes on the International Rule of Law." *Ethics & International Affairs* 28 (1): 53–64.

Fassbender, Bardo, Anne Peters, Simone Peter, and Daniel Högger. 2012. *The Oxford Handbook of the History of International Law*. Oxford: Oxford University Press.

Frazer, Michael L. 2012. *The Enlightenment of Sympathy: Justice and the Moral Sentiments in the Eighteenth Century and Today*. New York: Oxford University Press.

Goldsmith, Jack L., and Eric A. Posner. 2005. *The Limits of International Law*. New York: Oxford University Press.

Griffin, James. 2009. *On Human Rights*. New York: Oxford University Press.

Grotius, Hugo. 2004. *The Free Sea*. Indianapolis: Liberty Fund.

Grotius, Hugo. 2005. *Rights of War and Peace*. Books 1–3. Edited by Richard Tuck. Indianapolis, IN: Liberty Fund.

Grotius, Hugo. 2017. *On the Law of War and Peace*. Translated by Archibald Colin Campbell. Scotts Valley: CreateSpace Independent Publishing Platform.

Guzman, Andrew T. 2010. *How International Law Works: A Rational Choice Theory*. New York: Oxford University Press.

Hanley, Ryan Patrick. 2011. "David Hume and the 'Politics of Humanity.'" *Political Theory* 39 (2): 205–33.

Hardin, Russell. 2007. *David Hume: Moral and Political Theorist*. Oxford: Oxford University Press.

Harrabin, Roger. 2019. "Trump Confirms US Will Leave Paris Climate Accord." BBC News, October 24, sec. US and Canada. https://www.bbc.com/news/world-us-canada-50165596.

Hart, H. L. A. 2012. *The Concept of Law*. 3rd ed. Edited by Leslie Green. Oxford: Oxford University Press.

Hathaway, Oona A., Sabria McElroy, and Sara Aronchick Solow. 2012. "International Law at Home: Enforcing Treaties in U. S. Courts." *Yale Journal of International Law Yale Journal of International Law* 37 (1): 51–106.

Hobbes, Thomas. 1994. *Leviathan: With Selected Variants from the Latin Edition of 1668*. Edited by Edwin Curley. Indianapolis: Hackett Publishing.

Hont, Istvan. 2010. *Jealousy of Trade*. Cambridge, MA: Harvard University Press.

Hume, David. 1987. *Essays—Moral, Political and Literary*. 2nd rev. ed. Edited by Eugene F. Miller. Indianapolis, IN: Liberty Fund.

Hume, David. 2000. *A Treatise of Human Nature: Being an Attempt to Introduce the Experimental Method of Reasoning into Moral Subjects*. New ed. Edited by David Fate Norton and Mary J. Norton. Oxford: Oxford University Press.

Hume, David. 2006. *Hume: Moral Philosophy*. Indianapolis: Hackett Publishing.

Isiksel, Turkuler. 2016. *Europe's Functional Constitution: A Theory of Constitutionalism Beyond the State*. Oxford: Oxford University Press.

Kant, Immanuel. 1983. *Perpetual Peace, and Other Essays on Politics, History, and Morals*. Indianapolis: Hackett Publishing.

Koh, Harold Hongju. 1997. "Why Do Nations Obey International Law?" Faculty Scholarship Series, Paper 2101. http://digitalcommons.law.yale.edu/fss_papers/2101.

Krasner, Stephen D. 2002. "Realist Views of International Law." *Proceedings of the Annual Meeting* (American Society of International Law) 96 (March): 265–68.

Krause, Sharon R. 2004. "Hume and the (False) Luster of Justice." *Political Theory* 32 (5): 628–55.

Krause, Sharon R. 2010. "Moral Sentiment and the Politics of Human Rights." *Art of Theory* (October).https://www.berfrois.com/2011/04/moral-sentiment-politics-human-rights/.

Kumm, Mattias. 2005. "The Jurisprudence of Constitutional Conflict: Constitutional Supremacy in Europe before and after the Constitutional Treaty." *European Law Journal* 11 (3): 262–307.

Locke, John. 1988. *Two Treatises of Government*. 3rd ed. Cambridge: Cambridge University Press.

Lorca, Arnulf Becker. 2012. "Eurocentrism in the History of International Law." In *The Oxford Handbook of the History of International Law*, edited by Bardo Fassbender and Anne Peters, 1034–57. Oxford: Oxford University Press.

Malcolm, Noel. 2004. *Aspects of Hobbes*. Oxford: Oxford University Press.

Maniruzzaman, A. F. M. 2001. "State Contracts in Contemporary International Law: Monist versus Dualist Controversies." *European Journal of International Law* 12 (2): 309–28.

McArthur, Neil. 2004. "David Hume's Legal Theory: The Significance of General Laws." *History of European Ideas* 30 (2): 149–66.

McGregor, Lorna. 2006. "State Immunity Jus Cogens." *International & Comparative Law Quarterly* 55 (02): 437–46.

Morris, William Edward, and Charlotte R. Brown. 2016. "David Hume." In *The Stanford Encyclopedia of Philosophy*, edited by Edward N. Zalta, spring ed. http://plato.stanford.edu/archives/spr2016/entries/hume/.

Nickel, James. 2007. *Making Sense of Human Rights*. 2nd ed. Oxford: Wiley-Blackwell.

Nussbaum, Martha C. 2018. "Minimum Core Obligations: Toward a Deeper Philosophical Inquiry." May 11. http://jamesgstewart.com/minimum-core-obligations-toward-a-deeper-philosophical-inquiry/.

Paulsen, Michael Stokes. 2009. "The Constitutional Power to Interpret International Law." *Yale Law Journal* 118 (8): 1762–842.

Pavel, Carmen. 2015. *Divided Sovereignty: International Institutions and the Limits of State Authority*. Oxford: Oxford University Press.

Posner, Eric A. 2011. *The Perils of Global Legalism*. Reprint. Chicago: University of Chicago Press.

Postema, Gerald J. 1988. "Hume's Reply to the Sensible Knave." *History of Philosophy Quarterly* 5 (1): 23–40.

Ratner, Steven R. 2015. *The Thin Justice of International Law: A Moral Reckoning of the Law of Nations*. Oxford: Oxford University Press.

Sabl, Andrew. 2012. *Hume's Politics: Coordination and Crisis in the "History of England"*. Princeton, NJ: Princeton University Press.

Sagar, Paul. 2018. *The Opinion of Mankind: Sociability and the Theory of the State from Hobbes to Smith*. Princeton, NJ: Princeton University Press.

Sanchez Llamas *v*. Oregon 548 US 331 (2006).

Sayre-McCord, Geoffrey. 2013. "Hume and Smith on Sympathy, Approbation, and Moral Judgment." *Social Philosophy and Policy* 30 (1–2): 208–36.

Scott, James Brown, and William E. Butler. 2014. *The Catholic Conception of International Law*. Rev. ed. Clark, NJ: Lawbook Exchange.

South China Sea Arbitration, Philippines *v* China, ICGJ 495 (PCA 2016).

Tasioulas, John. 2013. "Human Rights, Legitimacy, and International Law." *American Journal of Jurisprudence* 58 (1): 1–25.

Tesón, Fernando. 1998. *A Philosophy of International Law: Human Rights Approach*. Boulder, CO: Perseus.

Guardian. 2017. "Burundi Becomes First Nation to Leave International Criminal Court," October 28, sec. Law. https://www.theguardian.com/law/2017/oct/28/burundi-becomes-first-nation-to-leave-international-criminal-court.

Tuck, Richard. 2001. *The Rights of War and Peace: Political Thought and the International Order from Grotius to Kant*. New York: Oxford University Press.

Verdirame, Guglielmo. 2007. "'The Divided West': International Lawyers in Europe and America." *European Journal of International Law* 18 (3): 553–80.

Vitoria, Francisco De. 1991. *Vitoria: Political Writings*. Edited by A. R. Pagden and Jeremy Lawrance. Translated by J. Lawrance. Cambridge, UK: Cambridge University Press.

2

Normative Judgment, Realism, and International Law

A strand of thought within international relations realism claims that international law, understood as the dense network of multilateral and bilateral treaties, customary law norms, and institutions tasked with interpreting and applying them, cannot have meaningfully legal authority. Since there is no centralized enforcement mechanism, international legal obligations can be ignored, especially when they clash with national interest. Far from serving as independent institutional mechanisms that constrain states, international treaties and courts are weak and only reflect existing power imbalances. States which act rationally to protect their interests must refuse to delegate power to courts as independent actors with legal authority to interpret international rules. For example, Stephen Krasner says that "for realism, the central admonition for policy makers is that they must make prudent judgments. They must assess the consequences of their actions. They can never rely on moral precepts. Applying law and judicial proceedings to international relations reduces the likelihood of prudential calculations" (Krasner 2002, 267). Krasner builds on a widely used rational choice model for state action to develop this insight. Its implication is that states are better off ignoring the constraints imposed by international courts and perhaps refraining from creating such courts in the first place. The substantive truth of the statement is a matter of considerable debate, yet in some ways even more puzzling is the fact that realists

Law Beyond the State. Carmen E. Pavel, Oxford University Press (2021). © Oxford University Press.
DOI: 10.1093/oso/9780197543894.003.0003

develop positions about what states "must" or "must not" do with respect to international courts and international law.

The distinctive contribution of my analysis is to show that realists' prescriptions about states' attitudes toward international law stem from deploying the rational choice model applied to states *prescriptively* rather than merely *descriptively*. The model of the rational egoist, initially developed for predictive purposes in economics, has proven to be a highly successful tool for modeling the behavior of individual and collective agents. With parsimonious assumptions about instrumental rationality, preferences, and choice situations, realists have put the model to good use to explain state action in the context of international politics. But they go much further, or so I will claim, by taking the unitary rational actor model to articulate an idea of states as moral agents with valuable preferences and goals and to prescribe the acceptable ways in which states ought to pursue those goals. Although present in realist thought only in rudimentary form, such a political theory of the state underpins much of realist thinking about international law. The parsimonious nature of the rational egoist model of agency for states means that it may work well for the purposes it was originally designed for, namely explaining and predicting state action, but its use for normative-cum-prescriptive purposes is illicit. There is substantial internal variety to realism, and the criticism only applies to some of its strands and not others. Therefore, I will focus on structural realism, which I find is especially vulnerable to this problem. I will show that structural realists put forward a distinctive, though hidden, political theory of the state.

Many contemporary realists think of themselves as social scientists and thus seek to produce explanatory theories that help us to understand and describe the behavior of states, international institutions, and other participants in international politics. This has not always been the case, and classical realists did not shy away from developing theories that combined ethical and empirical claims (Morgenthau, Thompson, and Clinton 2005; Williams 2008; Kennan 1966; K. N. Waltz 2001). But neorealism has adopted a stronger commitment to causal explanations and hypothesis testing in response to the perceived "unscientific" and moralized accounts of classical realists (K. Waltz 1979; Baldwin 1993; Rousseau 2002). Nowadays realists do not typically generate normative theories about *how states should act* but rather explanatory theories about *how and why states act* in certain ways. Normative theorizing is explicitly not part of the tools of social science. To see these realists conspicuously straddle the line between explanatory social science and normative theorizing raises an important challenge for them. They must elucidate how one can make the leap from explanations about how states act, to prescriptions about how states must act. In other words, they must justify how they go from a description of social facts to principles recommending (morally) right conduct.

One cannot go from factual premises to moral conclusions without making moral assumptions to motivate the conclusions. For example, we cannot argue that "one should not kill innocent people" (normative principle) without the moral assumption that human life is valuable, and that it is unjust to kill people who have done nothing to deserve it (say by being a threat). Similarly, one cannot argue that states should disregard international courts without assuming that such obedience is harmful, unjust, or morally problematic for states. My aim in this chapter is to explore both the ways in which realists draw normative judgments from factual assumptions about the nature of international politics and the types of unarticulated moral assumptions which help them get there.

There is a wealth of literature criticizing realist assumptions in international relations. Catherine Lu and David Welch have discussed at length the tensions between realists' prescriptive judgments and their core theoretical commitments (Lu 2011; Welch 2000; Sylvest 2010; Oren 2009). Catherine Lu shows that realists cannot defend the moral primacy of state interests without recognizing the necessarily shared foundations of states' right to pursue their private interests (Lu 2011, 44). David Welch criticizes the realists' overreliance on state or "national" interest as an explanatory variable, since "national interest is a vague and malleable term that can hide desirable or undesirable state behavior" (Welch 2000, 9). Ido Oren focuses on the apparent discrepancy between the realist commitment to "see the world as it is, not as we would like it to be," and yet to actively participate in criticizing or endorsing US foreign policy (Oren 2009, 283; Price 2008; Kertzer et al. 2014). The prescriptive use of the rational choice model for states is consistent with this claims and further elucidates why they are justified, but it persist as a problem that has yet to be diagnosed in the literature.

This analysis is of wider significance. The interplay between social science and moral theory is relevant to other corners of social science, such as political science more broadly construed, economics, and sociology, whose practitioners repeatedly find themselves in the position of giving advice to policy makers. I will argue that they can play this role responsibly only when they back up their social scientific claims with a defense of the moral acceptability of the policy goals they advocate for and of the means necessary to realize them.

INTERNATIONAL LAW AND REALISM

There are now more than 50 courts, tribunals, and quasi-judicial bodies in international politics that settle conflicts and interpret the rules of international treaties (Webb 2013, 1). These courts have issued thousands of binding rulings, 91% of which have been issued since the 1990s (Alter 2014, 4). Their decisions have helped states settle long-festering disputes, divide contested territory, and avoid the costs of uncertainty and conflict (Simmons 2002). Yet a political realist no less famous than Henry Kissinger has lamented the expansion of international judicial proceedings as encouraging the "tyranny of the judges," and the "dictatorship of the virtuous," which in his view inevitably leads to politically motivated prosecutions ("witch hunts"). To subject politics to law is to replace the political judgment and experience of national politicians with the judgments of international law and courts. This misguided faith in international law undermines peace and represents a radical departure from the existing practice of states (Kissinger 2001).

But subordinating politics to law is precisely what those who support the development of international law hope for. Relying on politics alone is a recipe for naked assertions of power, prejudice, and the pursuit of narrow state interest. International law can temper the pathologies of politics by balancing competing interests and serve as an essential facilitator for international cooperation. The various international treaties, agreements, and customs seek to minimize conflict and enable international agents to pursue individual and shared goals, and international rules and courts are central to this mission. For example, the law of the sea, based on customary norms and international treaties such as the United Nations Convention on the Law of the Sea (1982), offers various solutions to the competing claims states have over access to international and coastal waters, the exploitation of ocean resources, criminal jurisdiction, seabed mining, marine scientific research, and passage through straits of shipping and military vessels. It offers various dispute resolution options to member states, including access to an International Tribunal for the Law of the Sea. Most countries are parties to the convention and accept the jurisdiction of the tribunal.[1]

Realism is an internally varied research program, whose proponents and critics continue to debate the plausibility of its assumptions and the reach of its conclusions (Brooks 1997; R. G. Gilpin 1984; Lu 2011, 35–36). And realists tend to resist giving international law the status of a phenomenon worth acknowledging and analyzing; hence references to international treaties and courts are few and far between. Yet scholars such as Shirley V. Scott and Jens Ohlin have tied the reluctant attitude of the United States toward international law to the tenets of modern realism (Scott 2004; Ohlin 2014). Realists admonish policy makers to reject international cooperation in the form of treaties or use them strategically to seek power as a means of protecting national security (Scott 2004, 86). Powerful legal advisers for the US government have amplified realism in the corridors of power. In books such as *The Perils of Global Legalism*, they have argued that faith in international law is misplaced when it does not serve specific state interests (Posner 2009; Ohlin 2014, 10–13).

Realists assume a world in which states are unconstrained in their pursuit of self-interest. Thomas Christensen boils down the realists' insight: "[P]ower is what matters; and what matters in power is one's relative capabilities compared with those of others, especially other great powers" (2001, 10). This position often translates into specific advice for the United States's relationship with its potential competitors. In "Seeking Security under Anarchy," Jeffrey W. Taliaferro asks: "*[S]hould* the United States seek to guarantee its long-term security through a grand strategy of preponderance (or primacy) and pursue opportunities to weaken potential great power competitors, such as China?" (2000, 128; emphasis added). Both Christensen and Taliaferro are concerned that the United States might lose its strategic advantage in the face of a rising Chinese power and thus reduce its chances for influence and political domination.

This position can be traced to basic realist theoretical assumptions. John Mearsheimer gives foreign policy advice as well. States "must (therefore) act as rational egoists in what is a self-help world" (Mearsheimer 1994, 16). He says that "because states in a realist world are concerned about the balance of power, they must be motivated primarily by relative gains concerns when considering cooperation," the implication being that it would be wrong, foolish, or irrational for states to engage in cooperative dealing with other states that benefit them in absolute terms but do not benefit them as much as their counterparts in relative terms (Mearsheimer 1994, 12). In addition, he advises that "wars should not be fought for idealistic purposes, but instead for balance of power reasons" (Mearsheimer 1994, 48). By "idealistic" or "moral" purposes, Mearsheimer and Krasner rule out acting on reasons grounded in moral values (human rights) or rule-of-law reasons, such as submitting to and complying with the judgments of international courts. These are also ruled out by Eric Posner and Jack Goldsmith's view that "when the instrumental calculus suggests a departure from international law, international law imposes no moral obligation that requires contrary action" (Goldsmith and Posner 2005, 185). Realists share an underlying skepticism of the value of and compliance with international law and courts.

The fact that realists advise states to forsake international law when it does not further their own interests puts realists in the unique position of advising states to be outlaws in international politics. After all, even outlaws follow the law when it is in their interest to do so. This remarkable position is supported by a number of hidden normative assumptions. The next section describes the realist view and reveals the moral assumptions that form part of a distinctive realist political theory of the state. The following sections discuss why these assumptions are deeply problematic, a fact which counts against *realist prescriptions* for international law.

VALUE-FREE SOCIAL SCIENCE AND NORMATIVE REASONING

Much of international relations theory proceeds with the tools and aims of social scientific inquiry, and realism is no different.[2] Realists study the causes of peace and conflict, and one of their distinctive insights is that conflict is a pervasive feature of international politics. While classical realists such as Hans Morgenthau found the causes of conflict in human nature, or domestic politics, neorealists such as Kenneth Waltz argued that the primary cause of conflict can be found in the anarchic nature of international politics. The structure of international politics places severe constraints on state preferences and goals and determines the patterns of behavior of states away from cooperation and toward conflict (K. Waltz 1979, 62–73). Since realism asserts the dominance of the *structure* of anarchy in determining state behavior, it is often labeled *structural realism*. The main neorealist foil is liberal institutionalism, a view of international politics which claims that even starting with realist assumptions about the nature of anarchy and the preferences of states, one can explain broad and lasting patterns of international cooperation and state compliance with international law. International law and institutions move states away from a dynamic of conflict toward a dynamic of shared goals and peaceful relations. Cooperation to create international institutions and international law is neither automatic nor guaranteed to last once it happens. However, states do engage in cooperative behavior under certain conditions, and such behavior is beneficial for states. On the liberal institutionalist account, such a picture better accords with empirically observable regularities in state behavior (Keohane 1984; Oye 1986; Abbott and Snidal 1998; Martin and Simmons 1998).

Evidence of realist commitment to the social scientific mindset abounds in this debate. Miles Kahler explains that this trend toward more scientific explanations of international politics took a decisive turn with Kenneth Waltz, who "self-consciously aimed to produce a social scientific version of realism far removed from the anti-scientific model of power politics endorsed by the younger Morgenthau" (Kahler 1998, 924). David Baldwin, in an edited volume including leading neorealists and neoliberals, asserts that "the contributors to this [volume] share many fundamental assumptions about the nature and purpose of social scientific inquiry" (Baldwin 1993, 3). Similarly, Robert Powell, in an influential 1994 survey of neoliberal and neorealist thought, claims that structural theories, of which realism is one, are theories about how the units of international politics, namely states, interact with the anarchic structure of international politics. Such theories "try to make predictions about the units' preferred actions by combining assumptions about the units' preferences over outcomes with other assumptions about the structural constraints facing the units" (Powell 1994, 318). Joseph M. Grieco, a prominent neorealist, contrasts the competing hypotheses offered by neorealists and neoliberals and predicts that testing those hypotheses is "likely to demonstrate that realism offers the most effective understanding of the problem of international cooperation" (1988, 506). John Mearsheimer, another prominent neorealist, in his now famous article "The False Promise of International Institutions," argues that theories that offer alternatives to realism, such as liberal institutionalism, collective security, and critical theory, deliver causal explanations of the role of international institutions in creating peace that are not borne out by empirical evidence. Therefore these alternative explanations are mistaken in their causal logic in various ways (Mearsheimer 1994, 7, 19–26, 30–37, 42–47).[3] Needless to say, he believes realism does better on this account.

Realists' take on method accords with the naturalistic social science approach of a widely shared and respected view in political science. According to this view, the role of social science research is to build theories that "make valid descriptive and causal inferences" (King, Keohane, and Verba 1994, 3, 7). Gary King, Robert Keohane, and Sidney Verba describe scientific research as research that is "designed to make descriptive or explanatory *inferences* on the basis of empirical information about the world" (1994, 7). One does so by starting with a well-defined research question, constructing a theory that is specific enough to test the question, collecting valid data to assess whether the observable implications of the theory bear out, and making "inferences that go beyond the particular observations collected" (King, Keohane, and Verba 1994, 7, 28–33).

The raw material of social science theories is empirical observations. Theories produce hypotheses, meaning causal inferences about the connections among these observations. The hypotheses often contain descriptive assumptions that help to collect and interpret data. For example, a descriptive assumption is that states are unitary actors that act according to rational (means-ends) decisions about their preferences. Such assumptions need not necessarily paint a completely accurate picture of state behavior. Indeed, the assumption is controversial (Elster 1989, 177). Rather, the point of the assumption is to enable the theory to make testable predictions about state behavior. However, not all realists support the idea of testing theory against empirical data. In a paper coauthored with Stephen Walt, Mearsheimer has pronounced against hypothesis testing and in favor of developing better realist theory (Mearsheimer and Walt 2013). But he has not renounced the goal of realist theory as explanatory social science, and neither have other realists who engage in qualitative analyses of international politics.

One important consequence of the realist commitment to explanatory social science is that realists cannot engage in normative theorizing *as social scientists*. Ido Oren has shown that the realist commitment to the canons of social science that seek to observe, explain, and predict events is not compatible with intervening in these events by telling actors what they ought or ought not to do to bring about various outcomes (Oren 2009, 286–90). There are also philosophical reasons to be skeptical that realists can provide justifications for *how states ought to behave* from causal explanations and assumptions about *how states do behave*. Normative analysis must proceed from explicitly normative assumptions to normative conclusions, and realism is devoid of normative assumptions, or so it would seem.

Normative principles refer to principles that tell agents what they should/ought/must do in a given context or in general. Do not steal, keep your promises, do not kill innocent people are examples of such normative principles. The connection between normative principles and facts is such that facts cannot by themselves ground (or provide an exclusive justification for) normative principles. Facts, including social scientific facts (say about causal relationships among variables), are, to be sure, important to normative principles. Should I take an umbrella today? The answer to this question depends on a factual/predictive claim, that of the likelihood of rain. But the empirical possibility of rain cannot on its own justify the imperative that I ought to take my umbrella with me. I will need further reasons, grounded in the idea that I should avoid getting wet, and further, if getting wet makes me uncomfortable, I should avoid things that make me uncomfortable. Without this further, normative premise that health, or being comfortable, is good or valuable (however commonsensical it may be), there is no reason for me to take the umbrella, whatever the facts about the weather are.[4]

This example establishes a more general point: *normative conclusions about what an agent ought to do must be grounded in normative assumptions about what is valuable or morally required for the agent to have, aim at, or accomplish.* The upshot is that normative statements cannot be justified based on facts or social scientific explanations alone. The implications for value-free social science are straightforward. Scholars who engage in value-free social science cannot engage in prescriptive analysis about what individuals, states, and nonstate agents ought to do without relying on implicit or explicit normative premises about what is good, valuable, or worthwhile for those agents.

PRUDENTIAL AND OTHER NORMATIVE JUDGMENTS

Realists could claim that they are doing nothing as problematic as telling states what is good for them. When they advise that states "ought" to behave in one way or another, they are using the prudential "ought," meaning they take states' preferences as given and advise them on the best means of fulfilling those preferences. They are not using a moral "ought" and are therefore not guilty of sneaking in dubious normative assumptions about what is good, valuable, or just for states to have.

There are many versions of realism, as well as many varied assumptions and causal inferences drawn from them. I will focus in this chapter on a version of neorealism called *offensive structural realism*. Offensive realism is best captured by Mearsheimer in his seminal article "The False Promise of International Institutions." Mearsheimer claims that realism relies on five assumptions: (1) "the international system is anarchic"; (2) "states are potentially dangerous to each other"; (3) "states can never be certain about the intentions of other states"; (4) "the most basic motive driving states is survival"; and (5) "states are instrumentally rational" (1994, 10).[5] Realists thus rely on a standard notion of instrumental rationality or means-ends rationality: whatever an agent's ends or preferences may be, that agent acts rationally when she chooses the means that best help her accomplish those preferences. For realists, state preferences are always given and exogenous.

The assumptions taken in isolation predict at most that states will be defensive, Mearsheimer says. However, taken together, a different picture emerges: they create incentives for states to behave aggressively. Three patterns of behavior emerge. First, states fear each other, and they anticipate aggressive behavior from other states and therefore must always be ready for war. Second, because they cannot rely on the cooperative motives of other states or trust them as partners in security alliances, international politics is a self-help system. Finally, and most importantly, states aim to maximize their relative power over other states, which will drive them to take advantage of other states to increase their military capability and to prevent other states from taking advantage of them. That is, states will act offensively in order to assure survival. Cooperation is possible in this world, Mearsheimer says, but it is unstable and prone to breaking down due to cheating and states being concerned with relative military advantage even over their alliance partners. International institutions, and by extension international law, do not change the behavior of states; they merely reflect the existing distribution of powers among the states in the system (Mearsheimer 1994, 12–13).

In an article on the value of realism after the Cold War, Waltz underscores the radical nature of uncertainty in anarchic politics: "In the absence of an external authority, a state cannot be sure that today's friend will not be tomorrow's enemy" (K. N. Waltz 2000, 10). Realists believe that cooperation will be rare in a world without a global state, and that the anarchic structure of international politics pushes states into a spiral of threats and violence, in which "one state's attempts to increase its security appear threatening to others and provoke an unnecessary conflict" (Montgomery 2006, 151; Lake 2007; Rousseau 2002; Taliaferro 2000).

This realist world is presented as a series of descriptive and causal inferences about state behavior. Uncertainty breeds mistrust, and mistrust of other states' intentions leads to an exclusive concern with building up one's military capabilities, often at the expense of other states. Offensive realists predict more conflict and war than do defensive realists (Snyder 2002, 153). Defensive realists have different assessments of the probability of conflict, allow for a lower discount rate for the future and the pursuit of nonmilitary goals, and are comfortable with some coordination and cooperation as long as it does not significantly affect military capacity for self-defense (Brooks 1997, 447–67). Even Krasner is happy to concede that states cooperate to solve coordination problems, by establishing international communications regimes, for example (Krasner 1991). While defensive realists such as Waltz believe that states can be happy with the status quo when they achieve a balance of power with states that can threaten their survival, offensive realists believe that states only feel secure when they achieve relative domination, or hegemony (K. N. Waltz 2000, 6). For this latter view, radical uncertainty about other states' motives means that states are never satisfied, and a "spiral of hostility and arms races" characterizes the system (Rousseau 2002, 395; Jervis 1978, 197).

Offensive realists articulate an influential model predicting state behavior, assuming certain structural constraints of international politics. The model has severe critics, and many argue that the causal inferences that realists draw do not in fact follow from their descriptive assumptions (Martin and Simmons 1998; Keohane and Martin 1995; Wendt 1992; Powell 1994; Ruggie et al. 1993; Ashley 1984). I will leave such criticism aside. More important for the purpose of this analysis is the fact that realists believe that their theoretical conclusions justify certain *prescriptive conclusions* toward international law. In their view, international law and international institutions are detrimental to state interests, undermine the prudential calculations of state agents, are counterproductive, and make states vulnerable to domination by other states.

Mearsheimer and other realist feel comfortable making these inferences from realist models to normative prescriptions because they believe that certain prudential judgments follow from state preferences as realists understand them (Mearsheimer 1994, 49; Grieco 1988, 506–7). Their reasoning is of the following kind: given state preferences X, Y, and Z, states ought to do A, B, and C to realize them. But their prudential judgments are not merely prudential, because they are using instrumental rationality in a prescriptive rather than a purely descriptive mode. Hidden within the realist model of rational states actors are two normative assumptions: (1) it is good or morally valuable for states to follow their preferences, whatever those preferences are; and (2) that survival ought to be the dominant state preference. I will argue below that realists can get their policy prescriptions off the ground only if *the moral liberty for states to follow their preferences, and the ranking of those preference as realists see them, are defensible.* I will show we have reasons to question both assumptions. When the assumptions are challenged, the connection between realist models and their prescriptions for foreign policy and international law becomes much more tenuous.

THE NORMATIVE ASSUMPTIONS OF STRUCTURAL REALISM

It Is Good/Morally Valuable for States to Follow Their Preferences, Whatever They Are

Instrumental rationality or means-ends rationality posits that if an agent has end X, and A is the best means to accomplishing X, the agent ought to choose A. But it does not follow from this that the agent ought to accomplish X. At the extreme, take a state whose X is imperialistic conquest abroad and despotism at home.[6] Whether the state uses the best means at its disposal to accomplish its aims says nothing about whether the state should pursue them, whether scholars should advise politicians on the best means, or whether the citizens should support the state's actions. Therefore, we need a theory of morally acceptable state preferences and of the mechanism necessary to constrain states when they act outside of the range of socially acceptable behaviors.

Social scientists typically refrain from making judgments about the acceptability of ends. They either posit some ends or accept whatever agents subjectively affirm or reveal. According to instrumental rationality, agents cannot be irrational for preferring self-destructive, immoral, wasteful ends, or ends that harm other people. They can only be irrational for failing to take the means to achieve their chosen ends, whatever their ends may be.[7] That realists take state ends or preferences as prior and therefore as guides for state actions is revealed by the many admonitions that realists pass that states should not act in ways that damage their self-interest, which is a proxy for state preferences. Posner and Goldsmith, for example, say that "the states' obligation to keep promises is a prudential decision, not a moral decision. The decision to keep a promise turns on its effects on the good of the state" (Goldsmith and Posner 2005, 192).

Despite realists' protestations, this is a substantial moral position, not just a prudential one. It requires that states always put their interests first, even when doing so is harmful to projects shared with other states, such as upholding international law, or to the interests of other states. Realists can only advise that states pursue their interests if they believe that this is, morally speaking, the best course of action.

Relying on instrumental rationality alone leads us to the paradoxical conclusion that it may be wrong or immoral for agents to do what is rational for them to do. We can avoid this paradox if we observe that there are reasons for judging certain ends more acceptable than others and for preferring the ones that we have good reasons to affirm. While there may be no way to prevent agents from affirming the ends they do, other agents need not take those ends at face value, and indeed can actively work to ensure that social norms and institutions prevent agents from pursuing ends that are socially destructive. For example, individuals are constrained by law from pursuing socially harmful ends. States can also be constrained by international law from pursuing ends that are harmful to other states or to their own citizens. States can and should choose the ends and means that they have better reasons for pursuing when faced with a range of options. There can be such a thing as the "rationality of ends" in addition to the rationality of means.

Thus, in addition to a conception of instrumental rationality, we need a better understanding of what ends or preferences are acceptable for states to pursue. An analysis of states' proper ends goes beyond the aims of social science. Only if we make the assumption that it is good, appropriate, justified, or rational for states to have the preferences they do, including self-interested preferences, can we make the leap from describing states' preferences to advocating that states *should act* according to them.

This is especially important since states' preferences are tied to their fiduciary function as the protectors of their citizens' interests. States' authority is constrained by their mandate, and so are their preferences. States must not pursue ends which are severely damaging to their citizens' interests or survival. The acceptability of states' preferences will depend then on whether they reflect in part what is good, just, or valuable for their citizens. Realists cannot give states a blank check to pursue whatever preferences they happen to have unless they believe that any states' preferences should take priority over the interests of their citizens, the interests of people living elsewhere, and the norms of the international community.

Realists may deny that states "choose" preferences in any meaningful sense, and instead claim that state preferences are exogenously given. The anarchic structure of international politics, they claim, is what determines what ends states pursue. Exogenous preferences are a feature of their explanatory theory (Powell 1994, 317–18). But it is important to note that this is a big assumption of their theory, not a fixed fact about the world. It is a falsifiable assumption, and as Robert Powell observes, it is an assumption fit for certain theoretical purposes and not for others. In fact, Powell says: "the significance of taking the units' preferences as given in a theory or model depends very much on the theory or model and the purposes for which it has been constructed" (Powell 1994, 320).

Is there a sense in which states cannot choose their preferences? Maybe preferences are exogenous because states are not the kind of entities that can make choices about preferences. When Mearsheimer says that states must "act as rational egoists in what is a self-help world," he could mean 'must' in two senses. The first sense is that of a causal must without volitional choice: states "must" act as rational egoists because it is the only option available to them. In this case "must" indicates something close to physical necessity when all but one option for acting in conformity with one's goals are foreclosed.

However, a quick look at the context of Mearsheimer's claim is sufficient to rule out this special meaning of "must." States are acting, choosing agents and have a variety of behavioral options open to them, from altruistic behavior to moderately cooperative to rational egoist, and these options are not being closed off by anything resembling a physical constraint. So Mearsheimer would have to mean "must" in the second, prudential sense, of what is best for states to do, what is appropriate for them, what is required of them given their ends. And since he cannot go from a set of descriptive claims—states operate under anarchy, they are faced with uncertainty, they seek self-preservation—to a normative claim—states must act as rational egoists—without an explicit normative assumption that being a rational egoist is what states *all things considered* should be aiming at, he is sneaking in a normative premise about state rationality, namely that it is good for states to be rational egoists.

Furthermore, is it difficult to reconcile the idea that states cannot make choices about their ends with one of the main realist assumptions, that states are unitary agents which act according to instrumental rationality. If states can choose means, they can choose ends as well, since some ends are means to other ends. As Charles Beitz argues, scholars and state representatives ask "what states should do?" because states confront a variety of choices (Beitz 1999, 5). When states choose a course of action, they make choices about their goals and the best means to achieve them, and these are choices that depend on the agents' understanding of their context and of the moral norms that constrain them (Pavel 2015, 184–85). Thus, realists cannot have it both ways: if states can choose their means, they can choose their ends, too.

Realists unjustifiably restrict the menu of states' preferences to self-interested ones. As Jon Elster and others have observed, there are no good reasons to do so (Elster 1989, 52–60; 2000, 692; Brennan and Hamlin 2000, 6–10; Shepsle and Bonchek 1997, 17; Gaus 2007, 24–26; Parfit 1986, 5–7, 87–91).[8] Agents can have preferences about the well-being of other agents and can choose to act in ways that enhance others' welfare. Agents can also attach value to acts and processes, not just outcomes, such as conforming to social norms, following the law, doing what is expected or morally required, and so on. Amartya Sen has persuasively argued that "preference ranking for choice behavior may well be defined over . . . choice process . . . as well the outcomes at culmination," and has drawn on evolutionary theory to argue that people can attach intrinsic, not just instrumental, value to acts and conduct (Sen 1997, 747, 749). Agents may maximize outcomes (safety), but they may also maximize preferences over being cooperative or law-abiding, such that they will not consider increasing their security by breaking the law. Realists may want to argue that while this can hold true for individuals, it cannot hold true for states, but they will be challenged to defend the idea that states are different in this respect without giving up the idea of states as unitary, rational actors. States can have self-interested preferences, but also preferences for protecting the interests of other agents, including individuals and other states. More importantly, they may prefer to obey international law as a means to other ends or as an end in itself.

Realists tempted to suggest that self-interest and rule-following behavior are incompatible will have to resist that temptation. Most accounts of the emergence of social norms, law, and even morality emphasize that they developed precisely as technologies meant to enable different agents to accomplish their ends, whatever those ends might be (Kitcher 2011). Large-scale social behavior characteristic of modern societies had its early origins in the kin altruism and strategic reciprocity of earlier, smaller human communities, but went far beyond it, in patterns of intense sociability for which earlier forms of cooperation are a poor predictor. The evolution of social morality and of norm-guided human behavior has developed not due to altruistic motivations alone, but due to individuals' adapting to the constraints of their natural environment and, crucially, to the evolved expectations of their fellow humans (Richerson and Boyd 2006; Bowles and Gintis 2013; de Waal 1997; Gaus 2015). Such expectations have progressed culturally over time in sophisticated systems of positive social norms that guide the satisfaction of people's interests (Gaus 2011). Law is part of the system of positive social morality, and international law is a natural extension of existing positive moralities developed at the state level.

To sum up, states can and do in fact choose their preferences, and can do so having better and worse reasons for their chosen preferences as well as for their ranking. Therefore, states ought to follow their preferences only when they have good moral reasons for doing so. Good reasons include adequately protecting the interests of their citizens, not unduly interfering with the authority of other states, and furthering goals that enhance peace and effective coordination at the international level. Only once social scientists consider the adequacy of those reasons, are they in a position to provide normative guidance for public policy.

Even states which aim to be strictly instrumentally rational will be required to choose for themselves various rankings of ends, and in doing so they will cease being strictly instrumentally rational. They will develop a conception of what is good for them to have, aim, or accomplish. Suppose a state must choose among multiple policy options to punish an opponent. It can choose among military sanctions (intervention), economic sanctions (trade embargo, financial divestment), and cutting diplomatic ties (recalling ambassadors). Which of these sanctions the state will prefer will depend in part on what other goals the state aims to achieve, and thus on the cost of pursuing each policy relative to those other goals. Economic sanctions may be preferred when military sanctions can raise the level of instability and the state prefers stability, or cutting diplomatic ties may be preferred to the first two when the costs of military or economic sanctions for the initiating state may be too high and the state wants to preserve the economic status quo for welfare or military reasons. In choosing means, the state inevitably chooses a ranking of goals and thus a conception of its own good as an acting agent.

Therefore, a state can rarely refrain from making judgments about the ranking of its goals that will end up defining what is "good" for the state to do. Take a state with two goals, X and Y, and two means at its disposal for pursuing goal X, A and B, with A and B having differential impacts on the achievement of Y. In choosing which means to select for pursuing X, the state also chooses a relative ranking of preference of goals. Suppose the state must decide on pursuing X at time t1, but choosing either A or B means that the state will be unable to pursue goal Y in the foreseeable future. The state must decide if pursuing X is worth the cost of not being able to pursue Y. If the answer is yes, X will be ranked higher than Y in the preference structure. If the answer is no, the state must abandon pursuing X, and the preference ranking of goals reverses temporarily, at least until the time t2 when means C becomes available that makes pursuing X and Y compatible, and the state will have to reassess its preference ordering. Thus, in choosing means states often choose a preference ranking. These choices "define certain aspects of the content of the agent's good by setting out the sort of preferences that can or cannot be included in the agent's good-defining preference set" (Hampton 1998, 168). Choices about preferences and preference rankings are, in effect, moral choices.

Acting rationally means choosing from a variety of means to accomplish one's ends, but it also means choosing over time a conception of one's own good as an agent. In order to generate normative requirements, preference orderings for states must be defended, not simply assumed or asserted. Such a defense requires a philosophical argument about what the aims of the states ought to be or the range of acceptable aims states can have. The defense cannot rest solely on the fact that states as a matter of fact declare those to be their aims or act in ways that make those aims manifest. States can have aims that are immoral, detrimental to the interests of their citizens, as well as the interests of other states, and when this happens there can be no presumption that states should be able to accomplish what they want.

State Survival Is the Ultimate Goal

Preference orderings matter for what an agent should do. If an agent has the preference ordering X > Y > Z, with X being dominant, this means that the agent will devote relatively more resources to satisfying X than Y and more to Y than Z. Not only is state survival the dominant state preference for realists, but it is lexically prior to all other preferences, meaning the satisfaction of goal X—survival—cannot be traded for the satisfaction of goals Y and Z, such as economic development or a preference for cooperation. A different way to state this point is to say that X must be maximally satisfied before Y and Z are satisfied. Lexical priority is a mathematical term that was popularized in political philosophy by John Rawls's *A Theory of Justice* (1999, 266–67).[9] The insistence that survival is lexically prior comes from realists' claim that states must never accept an economic deal that is beneficial, if they lose in relative terms (meaning if they gain less than their competitors gain), because of the impact that a relative loss in economic benefits has on military capacity and hence on survival (Powell 1994, 314; Baldwin 1993, 7; Grieco 1988, 487; Mearsheimer 1994, 11–12). Again, realists move between a descriptive claim that states do not in fact accept cooperative deals where they gain in absolute terms but lose in relative terms, to a normative claim that states should not accept such deals. For example, Taliaferro's question of whether the United States should try to ensure its security by dominating and weakening China contains the implicit assumption that any deal with China in which the United States wins, but China wins more, is bound to have a negative effect on US security and should therefore be rejected (Taliaferro 2000, 128). This can only be true if the preference for security is lexically prior to a preference for economic development or for being recognized as a cooperative partner in world politics. This understanding of state preference ordering is highly problematic for a number of reasons.

First, lexical priority is an unreasonably strong assumption, especially when it comes to survival. One implication of the uncertainty and competition which realists maintain is inherent to international politics is that survival is constantly under threat, so a preference for survival can never be satisfied. This means that a state can never get around to devoting resources to other goals. If realists insist on lexical priority, they are in effect describing state agents with one goal only, that of survival. This seems implausible. States as collective agents have multiple goals, and survival can be at most one among many; it has to give way to others at least occasionally and likely often.

For human beings, survival is a biological given. But even for beings like us, the "commitment to the biologically given end of survival is not an all-or-nothing matter," as David Schmidtz puts it (1994, 237). People vary their commitment by degrees, and some individuals care very little about survival. For states, of course, survival is not a biological given. Then why are states committed to survival at all? Consider at least three possible ways to interpret state survival: (1) territorial integrity, (2) the preservation of the government in power, and (3) the preservation of state institutions as an expression of the collective right to self-determination. On some of these interpretations, state survival should not necessarily be a state preference. Territorial integrity may not be defensible when parts of a state's territory have been unjustly acquired, or when its citizens agree that it would be better to split it up into smaller self-governing units (as the former Czechoslovakia did). Similarly, dictators may have a preference for conserving their own power and will use state resources to ensure their will, but this does not mean that it is an end the state should pursue.

Disambiguating the meaning of state survival shows that survival is at most an instrumental value, and whether it has normative value depends on the higher ends it is an instrument for. State survival is conditionally valuable for safeguarding the citizens' physical security, welfare, or self-government, but not when it is used as a weapon by some citizens against others, by the power elites against the citizens, or against the lives and territories of the citizens of other states (Pavel 2015, 66–85). And not coincidentally, many of the conditions under which states can legitimately pursue their survival can be and usually are set out by international law.

As instrumental agents for the benefit of their citizens, states can pursue a range of goals, including goals that citizens invest their institutions with the authority to pursue. Among these are the protection of their citizens, trade, the peaceful resolution of disputes, and the promotion of human rights. Many if not most of them require states to comply with the demands of international law. Consequently, a proper understanding of state survival is not detrimental to compliance with international law and courts, but may require it.

It is as odd to suggest states should engage in the relentless pursuit of military security as it is to suggest that individuals should always devote their resources to physical security. Individuals divide their resources among a range of goals, including careers, education, traveling, raising families, volunteering, sports, and so on. We would think of those whose only concern is physical security as being in the grips of paranoid delusions, not as rational agents strategically pursuing self-interest.

Realists could of course reply that individuals in developed, peaceful states where survival is no longer a pressing concern have the luxury of prioritizing other goals. But international politics is a Hobbesian state of nature, and so the closest analogy to it is individuals in failed states. Realists do have a point, but it only takes them so far. During periods of intense, widespread conflict, individuals can focus on little else than physical security. But such periods subside. Even in countries mired in decades of instability and civil war, such as Somalia or the Democratic Republic of Congo, individuals go through long periods of relative peace, when they can move away from an exclusive focus on physical security toward engaging in trade, education, travel, and rebuilding infrastructure.

Realists will point out that the conditions for peace among states require a balance of powers or a global leviathan. Yet the "liberal peace" evidence shows that states can coexist peacefully in the absence of either of these. Liberal states do not go to war with one another, and this fact is explained by a variety of factors, among them representative government, a commitment to human rights, and economic interdependence (Doyle 2005; Russett et al. 1995; Danilovic and Clare 2007). These explanations rely on domestic and international commitments that liberal states make and as such reflect preferences or interests that these states develop, which in turn have effects on the dynamics of their interaction. A number of scholars, Anne-Marie Slaughter prominent among them, go further and argue that liberal states, as distinguished from nonliberal states, operate in a "zone of law" with each other. Due to their commitment to constitutional principles, the rule of law, and respect for the authority of other states, liberal states will be guided by principles of pluralism and mutual accommodation in their interstate interactions. By contrast, liberal and nonliberal states coexist in a "zone of politics," in which liberal states prefer to rely on political rather than legal means to solve disputes (Burley 1992; Slaughter 2000; Doyle and Carlson 2007). What states' relationship is to each other and international law depends on how they are domestically constituted and what preferences and interests they develop as a result of their constitution. For example, liberal democratic states are more likely to comply with their human rights treaty obligations, and when they ratify treaties, are more likely to have better practices overall, although the opposite seems to be the case for nonliberal countries (Hathaway 2001; Neumayer 2005). There is important insight in this picture of how domestic politics structures the attitude of states toward each other and international law. But as José Alvarez points out in a reply to Slaughter, the evidence for the claim that liberal states are substantially different with respect to their attitude to international law is more complex (Alvarez 2001). Many nonliberal states show high levels of compliance with international law, including in international economic law and the law of the sea, and liberal states have quite an ambivalent relationship to it, often stemming from the priority they give to their own constitutional rules and the concern they have toward the restriction of their ability to rule themselves if they submit to or comply with international law.

What this shows is that international law needs commitment mechanisms for both liberal and nonliberal states to resolve the fundamental tension between sovereign independence and the acceptance of mutually binding rules of behavior, and to create rules and institutions which further transform the relationships states have with each other away from war. The presence of more peaceful means of resolving disputes, via courts with compulsory jurisdiction, for example, is one way in which international law could encourage states to engage in more peaceful, rule-driven interaction, rather than interaction merely driven by political expedience, self-interest, and bias. If mechanisms to ensure more peaceful interaction via international law are available, to urge states to continue to prioritize their own military security, often at the expense of other states, is detrimental to most other goals they legitimately seek to pursue, and it involves an indefensible conception of the aims of individual states or of the international political order.

CONCLUSION

There is little justification for realists to claim that states should disregard and weaken the authority of international rules and the institutional mechanisms which interpret and apply them. Such a claim is based on a narrow conception of rationality deployed in *prescriptive rather than descriptive or predictive modes*. Together these features account for a distinctive political theory of the state hidden within the structural realist view, which prioritizes state survival above all other possible goals, including concern for other states and their citizens. This conclusion is not merely of academic interest. Realists are influential with policy makers. Insofar as we live with the policy choices that result from realist prescriptions and with their consequences, we pay the high costs and reap little benefit, or worse, we see the goals we care the most about undermined by such policies. Ultimately, realist prescriptions for international law will undermine states' efforts to resolve the paradox of commitment for states in international law.

The temptation to straddle the line between social science and normative theorizing exists because normative theorizing is vital. We want to be able to draw policy prescriptions that can guide us in the real world, and social scientists care just as much about getting them right as anybody else. Furthermore, we must aim to ground our reform proposals for foreign policy and international law in sound social science, but social science cannot on its own provide a complete justification for reform. We need a better appreciation of the values and goods that we are trying to achieve and how to handle trade-offs among them. Social science is vital in this enterprise (Wiens 2015). However, the analysis above makes clear the need to be mindful of its value and limits. Social science can provide causal theories, but it cannot tell us, all things considered, what *we ought to do*. Philosophical judgment must also play an important role, and the takeaway point is that social science and philosophical analysis need each other.

REFERENCES

Abbott, Kenneth W., and Duncan Snidal. 1998. "Why States Act through Formal International Organizations." *Journal of Conflict Resolution* 42 (1): 3–32.

Alter, Karen J. 2014. *The New Terrain of International Law: Courts, Politics, Rights*. Princeton, NJ: Princeton University Press.

Alvarez, José E. 2001. "Do Liberal States Behave Better? A Critique of Slaughter's Liberal Theory." *European Journal of International Law* 12 (2): 183–246. https://doi.org/10.1093/ejil/12.2.183.

Ashley, Richard K. 1984. "The Poverty of Neorealism." *International Organization* 38 (02): 225–86.

Baldwin, David A., ed. 1993. *Neorealism and Neoliberalism*. New York: Columbia University Press.

Beitz, Charles R. 1999. *Political Theory and International Relations*. Rev. ed. Princeton, NJ: Princeton University Press.

Blau, Adrian. 2011. "Rationality and Deliberative Democracy: A Constructive Critique of John Dryzek's Democratic Theory." *Contemporary Political Theory* 10 (1): 37–57.

Bowles, Samuel, and Herbert Gintis. 2013. *A Cooperative Species: Human Reciprocity and Its Evolution*. Reprint. Princeton, NJ: Princeton University Press.

Brennan, Geoffrey, and Alan Hamlin. 2000. *Democratic Devices and Desires*. Oxford: Cambridge University Press.

Brooks, Stephen G. 1997. "Dueling Realisms." *International Organization* 51 (3): 445–77.

Burley, Anne-Marie. 1992. "Law among Liberal States: Liberal Internationalism and the Act of State Doctrine." *Columbia Law Review* 92 (8): 1907–96. https://doi.org/10.2307/1123016.

Christensen, Thomas J. 2001. "Posing Problems without Catching Up: China's Rise and Challenges for U.S. Security Policy." *International Security* 25 (4): 5–40.

Danilovic, Vesna, and Joe Clare. 2007. "The Kantian Liberal Peace (Revisited)." *American Journal of Political Science* 51 (2): 397–414.

Doyle, Michael W. 2005. "Three Pillars of the Liberal Peace." *American Political Science Review* 99 (3): 463–66.

Doyle, Michael W., and Geoffrey S. Carlson. 2007. "Silence of the Laws—Conceptions of International Relations and International Law in Hobbes, Kant, and Locke." *Columbia Journal of Transnational Law* 46: 648.

Elster, Jon. 1989. *Nuts and Bolts for the Social Sciences*. New York: Cambridge University Press.

Elster, Jon. 2000. "Rational Choice History: A Case of Excessive Ambition." *American Political Science Review* 94 (03): 685–95.

Gaus, Gerald F. 2007. *On Philosophy, Politics, and Economics*. Belmont, CA: Cengage Learning.

Gaus, Gerald F. 2011. *The Order of Public Reason: A Theory of Freedom and Morality in a Diverse and Bounded World*. New York: Cambridge University Press.

Gaus, Gerald F. 2015. "The Egalitarian Species." *Social Philosophy and Policy* 31 (02): 1–27.

Gilpin, Robert. 1987. *The Political Economy of International Relations*. Princeton, NJ: Princeton University Press.

Gilpin, Robert G. 1984. "The Richness of the Tradition of Political Realism." *International Organization* 38 (2): 287–304.

Goldsmith, Jack L., and Eric A. Posner. 2005. *The Limits of International Law*. New York: Oxford University Press.

Grieco, Joseph M. 1988. "Anarchy and the Limits of Cooperation: A Realist Critique of the Newest Liberal Institutionalism." *International Organization* 42 (3): 485–507.

Hampton, Jean E. 1998. *The Authority of Reason*. New York: Cambridge University Press.

Hathaway, Oona A. 2001. "Do Human Rights Treaties Make a Difference." *Yale Law Journal* 111: 1935.

Jervis, Robert. 1978. "Cooperation under the Security Dilemma." *World Politics* 30 (2): 167–214.

Kahler, Miles. 1998. "Rationality in International Relations." *International Organization* 52 (4): 919–41.

Kennan, George F. 1966. *Realities of American Foreign Policy*. New York: W. W. Norton.

Keohane, Robert O. 1984. *After Hegemony: Cooperation and Discord in the World Political Economy*. Princeton, NJ: Princeton University Press.

Keohane, Robert O., and Lisa L. Martin. 1995. "The Promise of Institutionalist Theory." *International Security* 20 (1): 39–51.

Kertzer, Joshua D., Kathleen E. Powers, Brian C. Rathbun, and Ravi Iyer. 2014. "Moral Support: How Moral Values Shape Foreign Policy Attitudes." *Journal of Politics* 76 (03): 825–840.

King, Gary, Robert O. Keohane, and Sidney Verba. 1994. *Designing Social Inquiry: Scientific Inference in Qualitative Research*. Princeton, NJ: Princeton University Press.

Kissinger, Henry A. 2001. "The Pitfalls of Universal Jurisdiction." *Foreign Affairs*, July 1. https://www.foreignaffairs.com/articles/2001-07-01/pitfalls-universal-jurisdiction.

Kitcher, Philip. 2011. *The Ethical Project*. Cambridge, MA: Harvard University Press.

Krasner, Stephen D. 1991. "Global Communications and National Power: Life on the Pareto Frontier." *World Politics* 43 (3): 336–66. https://doi.org/10.2307/2010398.

Krasner, Stephen D. 2002. "Realist Views of International Law." *Proceedings of the Annual Meeting* (American Society of International Law) 96 (March): 265–68.

Lake, David A. 2007. "Escape from the State of Nature: Authority and Hierarchy in World Politics." *International Security* 32 (1): 47–79.

Linklater, Andrew. 1990. *Beyond Realism and Marxism: Critical Theory and International Relations*. Houndmills, Basingstoke, Hampshire, UK: Palgrave Macmillan.

Lu, Catherine. 2011. *Just and Unjust Interventions in World Politics: Public and Private*. Rev. ed. Basingstoke, UK: Palgrave Macmillan.

Martin, Lisa L., and Beth A. Simmons. 1998. "Theories and Empirical Studies of International Institutions." *International Organization* 52 (04): 729–57.

Mearsheimer, John J. 1994. "The False Promise of International Institutions." *International Security* 19 (3): 5–49.

Mearsheimer, John J., and Stephen M. Walt. 2013. "Leaving Theory Behind: Why Simplistic Hypothesis Testing Is Bad for International Relations." *European Journal of International Relations* 19 (3): 427–57. https://doi.org/10.1177/1354066113494320.

Montgomery, Evan Braden. 2006. "Breaking out of the Security Dilemma: Realism, Reassurance, and the Problem of Uncertainty." *International Security* 31 (2): 151–85.

Morgenthau, Hans, Kenneth Thompson, and David Clinton. 2005. *Politics Among Nations*. 7th ed. Boston: McGraw-Hill Education.

Neumayer, Eric. 2005. "Do International Human Rights Treaties Improve Respect for Human Rights?" *Journal of Conflict Resolution* 49 (6): 925–53.

Ohlin, Jens David. 2014. *The Assault on International Law*. New York: Oxford University Press.

Oren, Ido. 2009. "The Unrealism of Contemporary Realism: The Tension between Realist Theory and Realists' Practice." *Perspectives on Politics* 7 (02): 283–301.

Oye, Kenneth A. 1986. *Cooperation under Anarchy*. Princeton, NJ: Princeton University Press.

Parfit, Derek. 1986. *Reasons and Persons*. New ed. New York: Oxford University Press.

Pavel, Carmen. 2015. *Divided Sovereignty: International Institutions and the Limits of State Authority*. New York: Oxford University Press.

Posner, Eric A. 2009. *The Perils of Global Legalism*. Reprint. Chicago: University of Chicago Press.

Powell, Robert. 1994. "Anarchy in International Relations Theory: The Neorealist-Neoliberal Debate." *International Organization* 48 (2): 313–44.

Price, Richard. 2008. "Moral Limit and Possibility in World Politics." *International Organization* 62 (02): 191–220.

Rawls, John. 1999. *A Theory of Justice*. Rev. ed. Cambridge, MA: Belknap Press of Harvard University Press.

Richerson, Peter J., and Robert Boyd. 2006. *Not by Genes Alone: How Culture Transformed Human Evolution*. Chicago: University of Chicago Press.

Rousseau, David L. 2002. "Motivations for Choice: The Salience of Relative Gains in International Politics." *Journal of Conflict Resolution* 46 (3): 394–426.

Ruggie, John Gerard, Anne-Marie Burley, Judith Goldstein, James A. Caporaso, Lisa M. Martin, and Peter F. Cowhey. 1993. *Multilateralism Matters: The Theory and Praxis of an Institutional Form*. New York: Columbia University Press.

Russett, Bruce, Christopher Layne, David E. Spiro, and Michael W. Doyle. 1995. "The Democratic Peace." *International Security* 19 (4): 164–84.

Schmidtz, David. 1994. "Choosing Ends." *Ethics* 104 (2): 226–51.

Scott, Shirley V. 2004. "Is There Room for International Law in Realpolitik? Accounting for the US towards International Law." *Review of International Studies* 30 (01): 71–88.

Sen, Amartya. 1997. "Maximization and the Act of Choice." *Econometrica* 65 (4): 745–80.

Shepsle, Kenneth, and Mark S. Bonchek. 1997. *Analyzing Politics: Rationality, Behavior, and Institutions*. New York: W. W. Norton.

Simmons, Beth A. 2002. "Capacity, Commitment, and Compliance: International Institutions and Territorial Disputes." *Journal of Conflict Resolution* 46 (6): 829–56.

Slaughter, Anne-Marie. 2000. "A Liberal Theory of International Law." *Proceedings of the ASIL Annual Meeting* 94: 240–49. https://doi.org/10.1017/S0272503700055919.

Snyder, Glenn H. 2002. "Mearsheimer's World-Offensive Realism and the Struggle for Security: A Review Essay." *International Security* 27 (1): 149–73.

Sylvest, Casper. 2010. "Realism and International Law: The Challenge of John H. Herz." *International Theory* 2 (03): 410–445.

Taliaferro, Jeffrey W. 2000. "Security Seeking under Anarchy: Defensive Realism Revisited." *International Security* 25 (3): 128–61.

Waal, Frans B. M. de. 1997. *Good Natured: The Origins of Right and Wrong in Humans and Other Animals*. Cambridge, MA: Harvard University Press.

Waltz, Kenneth. 1979. *Theory of International Politics*. Reading: Addison_Wesley.

Waltz, Kenneth N. 2000. "Structural Realism after the Cold War." *International Security* 25 (1): 5–41.

Waltz, Kenneth N. 2001. *Man, the State, and War*. Rev. ed. New York: Columbia University Press.

Webb, Philippa. 2013. *International Judicial Integration and Fragmentation*. International ed. Oxford: Oxford University Press.

Welch, David A. 2000. "Morality and the 'National Interest.'" In *Ethics in International Affairs: Theories and Cases*, edited by Andrew Valls. 3–14, Lanham: Rowman & Littlefield.

Wendt, Alexander. 1992. "Anarchy Is What States Make of It: The Social Construction of Power Politics." *International Organization* 46 (2): 391–425.

Wiens, David. 2015. "Against Ideal Guidance." *Journal of Politics* 77 (2): 433–46.

Williams, Michael C., ed. 2008. *Realism Reconsidered: The Legacy of Hans Morgenthau in International Relations*. Oxford: Oxford University Press.

3

The International Rule of Law

> The rule of law is a moral idea, if we understand the word 'moral' as implying limits on the means by which governments as well as persons pursue their goals. Theories of law that ignore this moral element cannot distinguish law as a constraint on the exercise of power from law as an instrument of power.
>
> —T. Nardin, "" *(2008, 385).*

International politics as the realm of lawless anarchy has long been superseded by law-governed interaction among states. It reaches deeply into our ordinary lives, with rules regulating everything from trade in agricultural products, textiles, and services, to air transport, pollution, the exploitation of ocean resources, and scientific research. Moreover, it is sufficiently institutionalized to contain agents which make, interpret, apply, and enforce rules. The expansion of international law brings with it the possibility of arbitrary interference with the authority of states and the rights of individuals. Organizations such as the UN Security Council can authorize the use of coercive measures and even deadly force against any country or agent, without accountability or the possibility for review of their decisions. Imposing some restrictions in the form of rule-of-law constraints, which limit international law officials in their exercise of power, is desirable even for a young, incomplete system like international law.

Law Beyond the State. Carmen E. Pavel, Oxford University Press (2021). © Oxford University Press.
DOI: 10.1093/oso/9780197543894.003.0004

Examples of overreach or arbitrary power exercised by international organizations are not difficult to find. In the early 2000s, the Security Council (SC) adopted sanctions under Chapter VII of the UN Charter against individuals and entities who allegedly supported al-Qaida and the Taliban. The SC created a committee in charge of maintaining lists of individuals and organizations believed to aid and abet the terrorist network. It required all countries, including the European Union, to freeze the assets of those listed. In 2001 the SC committee added to the list Yassin Abdullah Kadi, a Saudi Arabian national and Swedish resident, and Al Barakaat, a Swedish charity for Somali refugees. Kadi and Al Barakaat brought suit against the EU for measures adopted in compliance with the sanctions, arguing that the measures violated their rights to property and due process. In a 2008 decision, the Court of Justice of the European Union ruled in favor of the complainants, explaining that the SC provided no avenues to access the justification for including particular names on the list, thereby denying the persons and organizations listed the possibility of challenging the measures taken against them. This constituted a violation of due process. Additionally, the court found that freezing financial and material assets without justification is an infringement of their rights to property. The judgment in *Kadi* is significant because it marks the first time a regional or national court argued that the SC measures violate fundamental rights (Zgonec-Rozej 2008). Although in Europe the application of the SC measures has been pushed back, they remain in force in much of the world.

As this example illustrates, given the extensive role it plays in regulating affairs among states, the potential for misuse or abuse of the authority of international law, and for inequities in the promulgation, interpretation, and application of its rules, is vast. An international rule of law must constrain the arbitrary power of public officials; impose discipline on the requirements about the formal qualities of the law, such as publicity, prospectivity, and coherence; and protect the basic rights of its subjects. My purpose is to persuade skeptics that the moral ideal of the rule of law has a place in international politics and to offer an analysis of its implications for international law.

Yet there is an important sense in which it is premature to talk about an international rule of law. Most of the rules of international law are only binding on countries which have signed the treaties that gave rise to them, there are no courts with compulsory jurisdiction, and the rules are openly flouted when they become costly or run counter to state interests. The consensual character of international law, which means that states are, for the most part, only bound by their consent, makes it more akin to a network of contracts between private entities than to the legal system of developed liberal democracies. Talk of a rule of law for the international realm cannot target law in the usual sense of the term, as a system of general, universally binding requirements, administered by an institutional system characterized by clear hierarchies and equal access to courts for the peaceful and fair settlement of disputes.

This chapter contributes a new perspective to the already extensive literature on an international rule of law, which is divided on the point or possibility of an international rule of law that mimics to the extent possible the features of a domestic rule of law (Waldron 2006; 2011; Besson 2011; McCorquodale 2016; Hurd 2015). There is wide agreement that the decentralized and consensual nature of international law, and the paucity of dispute resolution forums and of administrative and enforcement organs, means that domestic rule-of-law requirements cannot be simply transplanted to the international realm. For example, it is not immediately clear who the public officials of international law whose arbitrary power must be restrained are. The requirements of an international rule of law must be interpreted and specified for the very different context of international law. I argue that one of the main goals of an international rule of law is the protection of individual and state autonomy from the arbitrary interference of international institutions, and that the best way to codify this protection is through constitutional rules restraining the reach of international law into the internal affairs of a state. State autonomy does not have any intrinsic value or moral status of its own. Its value is derivative, resulting from the role it plays as the most efficient means of protecting autonomy for individuals and groups. Therefore, the goal of protecting state autonomy from the encroachment of international law will have to be constrained by, and balanced against, the more fundamental goal of an international rule of law, the protection of the autonomy of individual persons, best realized through the entrenchment of basic human rights.

The argument proceeds in several steps. I first provide an overview of different conceptions of rule of law, distinguishing between "rule of law" and "rule by law," and between thin and thick conceptions. Some of the most defensible strands of rule of law theorizing share the notion that the rule of law demands restraint on arbitrary uses of power and serves as an instrument for the protection of the equality and autonomy of the law's subjects. In this section I argue that thin or formal conceptions of the rule of law are incomplete, because they do not provide adequate constraints on legal systems to achieve equal protection under the law and the protection of autonomy of the law's subjects without relying on a substantive commitment to individual rights. I then discuss the implications of a thick rule-of-law ideal for international law, arguing that conceptions of international rule of law that defend it as an instrument for the exercise of state power as opposed to a constraint on the public uses of power are not acceptable. I then explain why it is important that international law protects the equality and autonomy of both states and individuals. I conclude with reflections on the institutional requirements of the rule of law in international law.

The implications of this argument for the legitimacy of international law ought to be clear. States often question the authority of international law on the grounds of actual or potential arbitrary interference with their sovereign authority, the unequal application of the rules, the lack of coherence between the rules of different areas of international law, and uneven access to courts for the peaceful resolutions of disputes. The state-centric bias of international law means that individuals do not enjoy an adequate protection of their interests and often lack legal standing to demand accountability for the abuses that states inflict on them. Strengthening the rule of law could go a long way toward enhancing the normative legitimacy of international law by giving states and other agents better reasons to comply with its demands.

THE POINT OF THE RULE OF LAW: THIN AND THICK CONCEPTIONS

Unlike other concepts such as liberty, equality, and democracy, whose value is regularly contested, the ideal of the rule of law receives near universal endorsement (Tamanaha 2004; Trebilcock and Daniels 2009). Closely associated with resistance to tyrannical government, protection of individual rights, and equality before the law, the idea of the rule of law took a historical hold in western absolutist monarchical states at the dawn of the Middle Ages and played an important role in their gradual transition to fully fledged liberal democracies (Tamanaha 2004, 15–32).

Rule of law captures what are commonly described as formal and substantive features of the law. Among the formal features, the most important are (1) generality; (2) publicity; (3) prospectivity; (4) stability; (5) capacity to reflect clear, reasonable, and mutually consistent demands on individuals; (6) proportional punishment; (7) easy access to courts; and (8) an independent judiciary. Formal features refer to the form and manner in which the law is promulgated rather than its content (Craig 1997, 467). These features require, respectively, (1) that laws must not single out groups or individuals, but rather be addressed to all, and ensure that no one is above the law, especially public officials; (2) that the obligations that law imposes are announced publicly, so that its subjects have reasonable notice of its demands and the opportunity to comply with them; (3) that laws are not retroactive, which would impede their ability to guide behavior; (4) that they are not changed too often, (5) that their demands cohere and they do not ask the impossible; (6) that violations do not incur draconian, disproportionate punishments; (7) that resort to justice is accessible to those who have been wronged, through a court system designed to facilitate speedy and equitable resolution of complaints, and (8) that justice is administered by officials free from political control.

Among rule-of-law scholars there is wide agreement that the rule of law embodies a moral ideal: it requires constraints on the arbitrary and tyrannical use of government authority for the sake of protecting individual equality and autonomy (Fuller 1969, 39; Hayek 1978; Hart 1984; Craig

1997; Dworkin 1998; Waldron 2006; Raz 2009, 210–33). Law itself must embody a moral relationship among the law's subjects, which means that no one person is exempt from the law or can exercise arbitrary will over another. Moreover, law's coercive capacity means that it must be applied with restraint, such that it does not unduly interfere with the subjects' life plans, and that it gives them opportunities to demand the accurate and equitable interpretation and application of the law and to challenge its violation. The rule-of-law ideal embodies both a horizontal relationship of equality among the law's subjects, such that no one subject has more power or authority over others, and a vertical relationship between officials and subjects, such that officials are constrained to respect the autonomy of the subjects. This is why the protection of individual rights is an essential feature of many accounts of the rule of law, in addition to the "formal" features.

A first important distinction legal scholars and practitioners make is between "rule of law"' and "rule by law." Brian Tamanaha thoughtfully points out that rule by law, or simply legality, sometimes masquerades as the rule of law. For example, China is happy to pay lip service to the ideals of the latter while avoiding many of its essential constraints (Tamanaha 2004, 92). "Rule by law" or *legality* describes government action guided by law as opposed to the personal whims or arbitrary will of public officials. Yet the content of the rules can be such that they authorize the government to unduly limit people's independence; to create and cement inequality between the law's subjects; and to immunize public officials against rules that apply to ordinary citizens, and against challenges to their authority. Rule *by* law is not rule *of* law, because it need not impose constraints on government power other than the requirement to remain within the bounds of the law. Rule by law can move a legal system away from the rule of law rather than closer to it.[1]

One of the main reasons China has rule by law but not rule of law is because it displays "rule-of-law" features imperfectly or not at all (Chin 2014). Any country like China that has general laws promulgated via a parliamentary and other lawmaking process, which guide both government's and citizens' behavior, whatever their content, can display some measure of generality, publicity, prospectivity, stability, and consistency. But generality requires that public officials are not above the law, which is plainly not the case in China. One of the major problems of the Chinese legal system is the fact that, due to the continued control of the courts by the ruling Communist Party, party officials are not accountable to generally applicable laws.[2] Legal professionals are routinely harassed, arrested, and tortured as a way to discourage challenges against government's authority (Pils 2017, 258; Haas 2017). Furthermore, the commitment to proportional punishment, equal access to courts, or fidelity to constitutional rules is at the best uneven and at worst nonexistent. For example, the constitution is vague, full of political slogans, and there is no provision for its enforcement, perhaps by design (Zhang 2012, 65). Rule by law does very little to restrain abusive government practices, especially when the content of the law is oppressive, or the law is applied without respect for due process: conviction rates in criminal trials near 100% and are often based on coerced confessions. In the latest Rule of Law Index (2016), a ranking that measures restrictions on government power, the protection of fundamental rights, and civil and criminal justice, China ranked 80 out of 113 countries, and limited progress in the past few decades on the rule-of-law front goes hand in hand with backtracking due to an increase in abusive legal practices (Chin 2016).[3]

As China's case illustrates, rule by law does not go very far in the direction of securing even the "formal" features of the rule of law. Moreover, the language of "formal" and "substantive" limits the proper understanding of the rule of law, since it gives the wrong impression that formal features are value free or value neutral. Some of the so-called formal features protect substantive values. The idea that no one is above the law, especially public officials, is a clear expression of a commitment to the moral equality of individuals. The idea of proportional punishment likewise embodies the idea of retributive fairness, which serves a more abstract notion of justice as giving people their due. The language of thick and thin conceptions of the rule of law better captures the idea that "formal" and "substantive" criteria are part of a continuum of rule-of-law features imbued with moral commitments.

Thick conceptions of the rule of law include requirements about the content of the law, not just their formal features. A list of basic individual rights is often considered a necessary requirement of the rule-of-law ideal, such as the right to life and to physical integrity, the right of due process, rights to freedom of action and of thought, and the right of private property. There are in fact two types of disagreements related to the substantive account of the rule of law: whether such an account is defensible, and if so, which rights are worth including. I do not have the space to fully defend the idea that individual rights should be part of an account of the rule of law, but a few reasons in its favor are worth mentioning. The first thing to say in defense of incorporating rights protection is that what is considered as merely "formal" rule of law is compatible with extensive tyranny. The "formal" requirements about generality, stability, and even equality before law will be incompletely realized and will offer limited protection against abusive government policies. The limited formalism achieved under Chinese law shows that rule by law is compatible with predatory laws leading to widespread expropriation, or laws whose role is to oppress and intimidate. Formal restraints are an important first step in constraining the government's use of arbitrary power, but are insufficient unless complemented by substantive constraints as well.

Second, it is hard to make sense of features such as equality before the law without individual rights protection. The point of insisting on equality before the law is to embody the fundamental notion that individuals are of equal moral worth, and the most secure embodiment of this notion is though the guarantee of rights protection. The point of the rule of law in limiting the exercise of political authority is to prevent regular abuses committed by governments against their citizens, such as unjust imprisonment, torture, violence, and large-scale oppression of political dissenters or minorities, and these are rightly seen as violations of individuals' and groups' fundamental rights. Rights violations are the reason government tyranny is seen as a universal bad and the reason for endorsing the moral value of the rule of law (Bennett 2011, 613).

But if individual rights are to be part of rule-of-law requirements, which ones ought to be included? Proposals range from basic rights—Friedrich

A. Hayek's suggestion to include the "inalienable, individual right of man" can be read this way—to Ronald Dworkin's full set of social and political rights (Hayek 2007, 63; Dworkin 1985, 11–12). The inclusion of all desirable political, social, and economic rights presents a serious problem, identified early on by Joseph Raz and H. L. A. Hart, namely that the more inclusive the concept of the rule of law becomes, the less it is distinguishable from other ideas such as justice or human rights, and the less it can be used as a concept that refers to the morality of law as distinguished from other normative concepts (Craig 1997, 468–69). This is precisely the ground on which Raz and Hart have objected to any thick/substantive rule of law ideal. They claim that (1) including substantive moral values such as individual rights requires a complete political philosophy; and (2) it would render the concept of the rule of law indistinguishable from other useful normative concepts such as democracy, human rights, or justice, and thus it would cease to serve its distinctive social function of providing a normative standard for evaluating legal systems.

We can reply to those like Raz and Hart that defend a thin/formal rule of law that the distinction between formal and substantive criteria is somewhat strained, as "formal" rule of law is based on substantive values such as equality, autonomy, fairness, and justice. As I noted above, many of the so-called formal features of the rule of law are grounded in moral commitments. Justice in the legal context is best understood not as the most encompassing political and social value, but as the demand that the law embody reasonable behavioral standards that are attached to proportional sanctions, fairness in the administration of the law, and equality of treatment before the law coupled with proper respect for and effective protection of basic rights. These are all contestable moral commitments, and supposing that focusing on the formal features of the rule of law avoids them misunderstands the rationale for having formal features of rule of law at all. The claim against Raz and Hart is not that "formal" rule of law is no improvement over arbitrary uses of the law, but that the ground on which to distinguish formal from substantive conceptions of the rule of law is weak, if it merely relies on the fact that formal rule of law avoids substantive ethical commitments. It does not.

The second concern is harder to dismiss, as turning the rule of law into the Trojan horse of all of the values we care about risks indeed making the concept indistinguishable from other substantive normative commitments that we resort to in order to pass judgments of justice and legitimacy. Raz and Hart are right that going the Dworkinian path takes us away from the rule of law understood as a moral ideal embodied in the law and closer toward a fully fledged theory of justice. One way to avoid this trap is to pack a minimal account of individual rights into the concept of the rule of law. For less than the full panoply of rights, the choice of what to include will be somewhat open ended, but at a minimum, it would have to count among its protections the security of persons and property, due process rights, and rights to freedom of action and expression. The open-ended nature of the basic rights necessary for a defensible account of the rule of law is an advantage, as it enhances the possibility to specify those rights through a political process where different states and groups negotiate and compromise, which will make them more likely to be accepted and implemented, and not through philosophical armchair theorizing. Nonetheless, if the more defensible conception of the rule of law is one that includes the protection of basic individual rights, what follows for the structure and practice of international law? The next sections are devoted to answering this question.

DO WE NEED AN INTERNATIONAL RULE OF LAW?

Eminent international law scholar and practitioner Martti Koskenniemi rejects the traditional ideal for the rule of law for international law. He identifies the rule of law ideal in the following way:

> The fight for an international Rule of Law is a fight against politics, understood as a matter of furthering subjective desires, passions, prejudices and leading into an international anarchy. Though some measure of politics is inevitable (as we commonly assume), it should be constrained by non-political rules. (2011, 36)

Far from endorsing the idea of the rule of law as a constraint on subjective desires and prejudices, and ultimately on politics, Koskenniemi seeks to reveal its conceit. Even though in this passage he refers to the weaker conception of the rule of law as legality, he believes that the idea that states can be bound by impartial rules is an unhelpful illusion (Koskenniemi 2011, 37–38). Ultimately, it obscures the fact that the principles of international law are contested, and thus disagreements can only be resolved via political means (Koskenniemi 2011, 43, 48–50).[4]

Yet is Koskenniemi working here with an implausibly strong conception of legal rules as uncontested and uncontestable, free of political stakes and consequences? The indeterminacy and contestability of rules is just as much a feature of domestic legal systems as of international law. And in the case of domestic law, we navigate indeterminacy by giving adjudicating institutions final authority to interpret the rules for specific cases and contexts. The indeterminacy of the rules can be reduced through a more precise specification of their content as well as through the procedures put in place to ensure adequate equitable and reasonable interpretation. It may be true as Koskenniemi insists, that "it is impossible to make substantive decisions within the law which would imply no political choice" (Koskenniemi 2011, 61). Legal decisions need not be politically neutral to be impartial in the legal sense. But from the fact that legal decisions have important political consequences in international law, it does not follow that law cannot exist in an independent, authoritative space which constrains political power.

Ian Hurd echoes this skeptical take by arguing that the domestic ideal of the rule of law cannot capture how international law works in practice. The international rule of law simply reflects the way in which states use law to justify and pursue foreign policy (Hurd 2015, 367). The concepts of domestic and international rule of law arose in response to different problems. The point of domestic rule of law is to place limits on the exercise of centralized power and to protect the equality of citizens, while the point of the international rule of law is to respond to the lack of a centralized international authority and to cement the consensual character of law among states (Hurd 2015, 366–67).

For Hurd, both the purposes and the institutional requirements of the international rule of law must be different from those of the domestic rule of law; international law regulates relations among states, while domestic law regulates relations among individuals and other nonstate agents. The implication of this difference for Hurd is that the international rule of law must affirm the instrumental role international law plays in serving state interests. Each state has a different constellation of obligations, and states will use international law to justify and legitimate their actions. He claims that "in the interstate setting, this goal of a unified set of public rules that applies to all subjects cannot be achieved or even approximated because states retain the authority to accept, reject, or modify their legal obligations through treaty accession, reservations, and persistent objections" (Hurd 2015, 382). Therefore, the universally biding character of domestic law cannot be a feature of international law, and therefore many of the characteristics of the domestic rule of law that come with it, such as equality before the law, must be abandoned.

Hurd makes a good case that the steady and large amount of formalization of the relations between states through treaties constitutes a big step in the direction of rule-governed interaction, as opposed to leaving them to the vagaries of politics, power imbalances, and prejudice (Hurd 2015, 378). Codification brings with it the important formal features of the rule of law, such as clarity, predictability, prospectivity, and coherence, and creates the basic rules that structure the relations among states. The international order is "constitutional" in Hurd's view, in the sense that it generates rules that explain how states can make treaties and the ways in which those treaties create responsibilities for them. But it is not "constitutional" in the more traditional sense in which it protects certain fundamental rights of the law's subjects against encroachment by its institutions.

This position is deeply problematic if an international rule of law is understood simply as a vehicle for facilitating the realization of state interests. Hurd is right that the different structure and purposes of international law mean that its institutional requirements must be different. But he is wrong to equate the rule of international law with legality, or "rule by law." First of all, his approach fails to take the rule of law seriously as a moral ideal whose primary function is to place constraints on the exercise of power by subjects against one another and by political authority against subjects. As Terry Nardin (2008, 385) aptly observes, this position belongs to a class of international relations views that fail to distinguish law as an instrument of power from law as a constraint on power. Hurd is repeating the common refrain among international relations scholars that since the circumstances of international anarchy make it impossible to realize uniform, enforceable law among states, international law must be by necessity an instrument of state foreign policy rather than a common instrument for solving public goods problems or for achieving peace or justice. There is no distinction in this view between law and mere power.

Law is not only distinct from power but must be the antithesis of power if it is to serve its social purpose properly. Law must constrain the power that individuals exercise over one another for the sake of peaceful coexistence; it must recognize and protect their equal moral status; and it must assist them in the pursuit of individual and common ends, including public goods. And above all, law must constrain the exercise of power by public officials. The ideal rule of law is one of the ways in which law instantiates these values. While it is perfectly possible to have law as a set of primary rules that direct subjects about appropriate standards of behavior which lacks many of these features, no system of law is merely instrumental and serves solely the purpose of affirming the power and interests of its subjects. Mere instrumentality is actually impossible to realize, since the law's subjects exercise their power in ways that threaten each other's survival and limit the pursuit of each other's interests. International law cannot be merely an instrument of state power simply because different states may wish to pursue conflicting and mutually exclusive ends, and the role of international law is to limit the ways in which states can harm each other and their citizens in pursuit of these ends, while protecting a sphere of autonomous action for states and individuals.

International law has distinctive substantive and structural features, ill-suited at least for now to some of the common ways to implement the domestic rule of law. The strong consensual element of international law means that states are for the most part only bound by treaties and rules they explicitly agree to. The implication of this feature is that very few international rules, with the exception of the UN Charter, customary law, and the decisions of the Security Council, bind everyone. This means that equality before the law is limited under treaty law to states that accede to a particular treaty.[5] For example, treaties protecting various human rights bind only the states that have ratified them, and the statute creating the International Criminal Court binds the states that have become members of the court, unless the Security Council refers a nonmember state to the Court for investigation.

This makes the character of international law different from domestic law, where law binds individuals with or without their consent. While domestic law can also distinguish between subjects based on consent, say due to the law of contract, it typically contains a large number of legal rules which apply regardless of subjects' consent, including those restricting the use of violence, granting due process rights, or subjecting public officials to generally applicable law, and thus equality before the law means that individuals are subjected to laws with general applicability, and that they possess equal rights and obligations. By contrast, states' obligations vary with their willingness to commit to certain rules and not others. It is a point of contention that states are divided between those whom the ICC can reach and those whom it cannot, and it certainly cannot touch the permanent members of the Security Council who are not members and will refuse to self-refer to the court.

Equality before the law is necessary even in a legal system such as international law, because under a consent-based system, powerful states often manage to extricate themselves from their obligations to respect even the least intrusive general rules, such as noninterference with the sovereign prerogatives of other states, and from rules that should have a more general character, such as the international rules for criminal accountability. Consent cannot be determinative of states' rights and obligations in a world in which political officials often misrepresent their citizens' interests by withholding consent from rules that could better protect these interests, at least in the case of nondemocratic/authoritarian states. The normative significance of state consent is weakened by its ability to divide the world into those to whom the rules apply and those to whom they do not.

We should acknowledge with Hurd that legalization is an important step toward the implementation of the rule of law. Nonetheless, it cannot constitute the endpoint of efforts to build the rule of law. An ideal of an international rule of law can inform efforts to reform the current system to reduce power asymmetries and put guarantees in place to ensure a more even distribution of rights and responsibilities among states. Unless one believes that feasibility constraints for an international rule of law are so great that they disqualify it as a goal worth pursuing, we should consider possible avenues for reform in international law that place limits on the arbitrary use of power, defend the equality and autonomy of individuals, and bind public officials to generally recognized rules. It is difficult to contemplate at this point in time a world in which states have stronger and equal obligations under international law, given that states have a propensity to guard their sovereign prerogative jealously. Yet the domestic rule of law developed as a response to similar circumstances, in which individuals and groups enjoyed unequal status and power; there was no unified system of rules that applied to all; and legal rules lacked generality, coherence, or fairness in their application.

The rule of law for domestic law was an achievement many centuries in the making, and it started from structural background conditions not very different than the ones present in international law today. Douglass North, John Joseph Wallis, and Barry R. Weingast argue that the formation of modern states can be best understood as evolving from "natural state" political orders, characterized by legal compromises among the powerful, dominant individuals, who agreed to respect each other's privileges, including rights to territory and resources, and restrict their use of violence. "Natural orders" were not inclusive, open, social orders because these privileges did not extend equally to the less powerful and more vulnerable members of the society in the same way that they do today in liberal democratic societies (North, Wallis, and Weingast 2013, 18–21, 30–76). States today rely on international law to protect their sovereign authority and territory, but at the same time insulate themselves from rules the more powerful they are, which leaves the less economically and militarily powerful states vulnerable to abuse. The former can withhold consent to international treaties that impose serious restrictions on their capacity to act, while the latter are limited in their capacity to use international law to limit violations of their rights and to protect their interests. Hierarchy, status, and raw power are as much characteristics of international law today as they are of natural orders that characterized early state formation.[6]

International law in its current form is a rule *by* law system in which the officials in the system are guided by rules in their interaction, rather than a rule *of* law system, which constrains the most powerful actors, and under which legal subjects enjoy equality before the law. Rule *by* law is not acceptable as the ultimate expression of the rule of law because it does not achieve the aims of the rule of law, which are protecting the autonomy of the subjects and restraining the arbitrary use of power. While some existing features of international law will make it difficult to move beyond a consensual "rule by law" framework, these features could be changed gradually to move international law toward a stronger rule-of-law system. Setting up general rules, expanding the number and reach of courts that give both states and individuals access to impartial dispute settlement, and creating more effective systems of enforcement are achievable given the rapid legalization of international politics today.

Therefore, an approach that takes the international rule of law as a moral ideal seriously requires the strengthening of features that circumscribe the authority of public officials and protect individual and state autonomy. Of the eight "formal" features—(1) generality; (2) publicity; (3) prospectivity; (4) stability; (5) capacity to reflect clear, reasonable, and mutually consistent demands on individuals; (6) proportional punishment; (7) easy access to courts; and (8) an independent judiciary—only (2); (3) (4) and to some extent (5) are realized in international law. The increasing legalization of the relations among states means that more of their interactions and disagreements are governed by rules laid out in advance, that are relatively clear, stable, and public. But generality is not yet a feature of international law, nor is easy access to courts, despite the rise in the number of international courts and tribunals. States are still the main subjects in international law, and they alone have standing to bring claims to most international courts. Furthermore, their legal standing has no effect when another state party to a dispute rejects the jurisdictional authority of an international court. Punishment for violations of international law is limited, which means proportional punishment is not yet a feature of rule-governed interaction among states. International law has been described as a self-help system, and that description still applies today to large swaths of international law (Kelsen 1952, 14).

THE PURPOSE OF THE INTERNATIONAL RULE OF LAW

In the absence of a bureaucratic structure that closely resembles a world government, two questions arise: (1) Which agents have the potential to exercise arbitrary power that must be limited? and (2) Who are the subjects of international law whose autonomy must be protected from arbitrary interference? The answer to the second question is more straightforward. International law is addressed mostly to states, with an increasing but still small role for individuals and other group and corporate agents—companies, indigenous groups, nongovernmental organizations (NGOs)—as direct subjects of international law. An international rule of law would need to protect all of these agents, as well as any other actors that would fall under its remit directly or indirectly through the mediating power of states, from arbitrary power exercised by global governance institutions and international officials in their exercise of their capacities.

The answer to the first question is that all of the agents that make, interpret, and apply international law can potentially exercise arbitrary power that must be limited. These are primarily states, who have the power to make treaties, and the international institutions that states endow with autonomous capacity to apply and enforce the rules, such as the International Court of Justice, the World Trade Organization, various ad hoc tribunals and regional courts and organizations, and the agencies of the United

Nations system, including the Security Council. Thus states have a dual agency both as subjects and officials of international law.

The idea that international law should be promulgated and constrained such that it protects state autonomy is very much in dispute. Jeremy Waldron argues that the protection of state autonomy should not be one of the aims of an international rule of law (Waldron 2006, 18). He draws an analogy with domestic law, for which he distinguishes two general subjects, individuals and administration, and argues that only individuals are entitled to the benefit of the rule of law and the protection of their autonomy. The rule of law creates a predictable environment in which individuals exercise their freedom and plan their lives secure in the knowledge that no arbitrary use of state power will undo their plans at will. Administration, by which he means the collection of government bureaucratic bodies, holds no entitlement to the protection of its autonomy from the law in the same way. Whereas less law is better for individual autonomy, no such presumption is warranted with respect to administration. In fact, more law is required to regulate administrative bodies rather than less, because this means that more of their actions are taken in accordance with rules laid out in advance and that their discretion is limited accordingly (Waldron 2006, 18–19).

As officials in charge of making international law, states are in the same position as domestic administration, Waldron claims. Their behavior must be constrained and their discretion limited by more law, not less, and they do not gain the presumption in favor of the protection of their autonomy. States are constituted as legal entities of international law, and their autonomy does not rest on a fundamental normative principle in the same way that individual autonomy does in domestic law (Waldron 2006, 23; 2011, 339).

But is it true that international law should not protect state autonomy? What would be the consequences of extensive regulatory intrusion of international law into member states, with no limit on the ability of international law to regulate or change national laws and to create differential protections and privileges for different states such that the autonomy of some is protected but not of all? To some extent this is the current reality of international law, with the permanent members of the Security Council exercising disproportionate power over other states and enjoying some measure of immunity from the rules that these other states are subjected to. Indeed, as Anthony Anghie has said, it is plausible to argue that the Security Council divides the world into two: those to whom the rules do not apply (the five permanent members), and those to whom they do.[7] Antoinette Scherz and Alain Zysset propose that enhancing the normative legitimacy of the Security Council requires reforming the membership structure, although any substantial reforms will meet with serious resistance (Scherz and Zysset, 13–15). Nonetheless, without such reforms, the imbalance of power at the Security Council seriously affects the fairness and legitimacy of international law as a whole, and the practical consequence of this imbalance can be a significant loss to the value of democratic self-determination within states. It opens the possibility of such severe erosion of sovereignty and all of the values it protects (independence from others, local rule, diversity of political and institutional cultures) that it raises questions about the legitimacy of international law as a whole. The existing institutional setup could end up denying states the liberty of pursuing diverse goals, and it would misdirect the power of international law in an oppressive, paternalistic direction (Nardin 1983).

States are entitled to autonomy not for their own sake, but for the sake of the individuals they represent and govern. Thus, the value of state autonomy rests on the value of individual autonomy as a fundamental normative commitment, and in this sense, it is derivative. States' interest in autonomy is important because it protects individual and collective self-determination. As officials of international law, we can insist that states should be rule bound in their lawmaking capacity. But as subjects of international law, states are entitled to a wide berth to make decisions in line with the collective wishes of their populations, and the fact that state autonomy is instrumentally valuable does not mean it carries little weight. Precisely because of its role in protecting individual autonomy, state autonomy under international law should enjoy the widest presumption. At the same time, states are not entitled to unlimited autonomy. State autonomy must be limited for the sake of other states' autonomy and the autonomy of individuals who are their own citizens or the citizens of other states. For example, international law cannot legitimate a state interfering in the autonomous decisions of other states, even if that interference has been justified via internal democratic processes. Limitations on state autonomy are justified in the name of severe violations of individual autonomy, of other states' autonomy, of solving cooperation problems such as public goods and collective action dilemmas, and in the interest of international peace and order.

Waldron quotes Abram Chayes approvingly to suggest that as mere officials of international law, states must be bound by law and are not entitled to respect for their autonomy: "[I]f states are the 'subjects' of international law, they are so, not as private persons are the 'subjects' of municipal legal systems, but as government bodies are the 'subjects' of constitutional arrangements' (Waldron 2011, 328). But this position does not follow from a proper description of states as both *subjects and officials* of international law. As lawmakers, states are subject to international law as governmental bodies are subject to constitutional arrangements. But as addressees of the law, they must be granted wide protections for their autonomous lawmaking capacity internally.

States are not the only officials of international law. International lawmaking organizations, including international courts, must exercise their powers through laws that are prospective, general, stable, and reflect demands that are reasonable and compatible with each other, and whose operation is independent of political influence and can provide easy access for the law's subjects, whether states, individuals, or other agents operating in international politics.

State autonomy is valuable to the extent it protects individual autonomy. The protection of individual autonomy in international law can be realized through the protection of basic human rights and through rules that prevent states and international organizations from unduly interfering with the ability of individuals to exercise their freedom and plan their lives. This is in effect the primary goal of an international rule of law, compatible with understanding states as agents of their people and acting on their behalf. International law must protect individuals from their own states, other states, or agents, and states from each other and from international institutions (Waldron 2011, 324).

THE INSTITUTIONAL CONTOURS OF THE INTERNATIONAL RULE OF LAW

Both states and individuals enjoy some degree of rights protection in international law. States benefit from rights of noninterference with their sovereign authority and limited rights of sovereign equality under the rules of the UN Charter, while individuals benefit from an extensive network of human rights treaties. But there are still many unresolved conflicts among the rights of states and between the rights of states and those of individuals, as debates about the permissibility of humanitarian intervention or limits on sovereign immunity illustrate (Nardin and Williams 2005; Pattison 2012; Knuchel 2010).

Realizing the moral ideal of the rule of law in international law requires institutional reform. At the very minimum, we should move in the direction of creating some universally binding rules and courts with compulsory jurisdiction, which guarantee better access by all of the subjects of international law to the resolution of grievances and the peaceful settlement of conflicts.

Many if not all of the institutions and courts operating in international law, that contribute to making, interpreting, and applying rules, and adjudicate conflicts, including the World Trade Organization, the International Criminal Court, and the Law of the Sea Tribunal, carry the potential to abuse their authority, and currently they face little oversight. Correcting this significant shortcoming of international law requires rules that specify in detail the limits of the authority delegated to international governance institutions and empower agents to check each other and to render judgment over arbitrary exercises of authority. The international rule of law demands more than oversight and accountability ensured through institutional checks and balances. It demands that equality before the law be strengthened and the protection of basic interests of the participant in the international order be made explicit through a list of rights and entitlements that receive special status as fundamental building blocks of an international legal order.

There are various institutional alternatives for building these features of the international rule of law, but one that merits attention is a constitutional international order. A constitutional international order defines the division of authority between international institutions and states, prescribes rights of noninterference for states, and enumerates basic individual rights deserving special weight in the making, interpretation, and application of international law.

The way to solve the problem of states opting out of the morally required minimum of law is to create bodies with the power to create international law that applies universally, evenly, and efficiently. For example, giving the ICC jurisdiction over crimes committed by the citizens of all states, not just member states, would be a step forward in this direction. Indeed, as Thomas Christiano argues, it is hard to see the exclusion of some of the most powerful states from its jurisdiction as something other than a bold attempt to place themselves above international law (Christiano 2020, 356–361). States could adopt universally binding rules via some form of constitutionalization, which would spell out some minimal, binding obligations and rights for states, individuals, and other subjects of international law. Constitutionalization can preserve a substantial level of autonomy for individual states. The point of a constitutional order is to make sure that it does precisely this.

An account of the constitutionalization of international law will be developed further in Chapter 5. However, other scholars have already offered instructive insights. Christian Tomuschat describes an international constitution as "a legal framework of limited number of basic rules" to constrain states "which determines their basic rights and obligations with or without their will" (1993, 211). Judge James Crawford, who has served at the International Court of Justice, defends a constitutional order which involves constraints on state powers and on international institutions and guarantees for rights (2014, 455, 460–61, 466). He argues that the process of constitutionalization should build on the emerging hierarchy in international law, that places the UN Charter with its the restriction on the use of force of at its core, along with jus cogens norms and obligations erga omnes (Crawford 2014, 465–66).

While a global constitutional order would constitute a substantive, qualitative transformation of the relationship of national to international law, such a transformation would not be wholesale. Global constitutionalism could still preserve the largely consensual nature of international law but make changes in the direction of creating universally binding law. These changes will alter the relationship of states to international law on a number of crucial issues, and we can insist international law does so only for those issues, to avoid overreach and the disabling of state sovereignty.

The road to an international constitutional order will be long and hard, fraught with resistance from states and international organizations alike, and punctuated by difficult choices about the precise content of the constitutional rules. But it marks one of the surest ways to ensure the strengthening of international rule of law. Building the rule of international law represents an important avenue for enhancing the legitimacy of international law, by giving states and individuals better reasons to comply with its demands. For example, global constitutional norms which limit the authority of international law, mandate or proscribe certain behaviors for all subjects, and create courts with universal compulsory jurisdiction can stave off concerns with arbitrary interference with state sovereignty, the unequal application of the rules, and the lack of access to courts for the peaceful resolution of disputes. A global constitution can address all of the existing limitations of international law in this respect while protecting an important sphere of autonomous state action. And it can do so consistent with a fundamental commitment to respect the basic rights of individuals on behalf of whom states exercise their authority.

REFERENCES

Bennett, Mark J. 2011. "Hart and Raz on the Non-Instrumental Moral Value of the Rule of Law: A Reconsideration." *Law and Philosophy* 30 (5): 603–35.

Besson, Samantha. 2011. "Sovereignty, International Law and Democracy." *European Journal of International Law* 22 (2): 373–87.

Christiano, Thomas. 2020. "The Arbitrary Circumscription of the Jurisdiction of the International Criminal Court." *Critical Review of International Social and Political Philosophy* 23 (3): 352–70.

Chin, Josh. 2014. "'Rule of Law' or 'Rule by Law'? In China, a Preposition Makes All the Difference." *Wall Street Journal*, October 20. https://blogs.wsj.com/chinarealtime/2014/10/20/rule-of-law-or-rule-by-law-in-china-a-preposition-makes-all-the-difference/.

Chin, Josh. 2016. "China Lags Behind in Rule-of-Law Ranking." *Wall Street Journal*, October 20. https://blogs.wsj.com/chinarealtime/2016/10/20/china-lags-behind-in-rule-of-law-ranking/.

Craig, Paul P. 1997. "Formal and Substantive Conceptions of the Rule of Law: An Analytical Framework." *Public Law*, 467–87.

Crawford, James. 2014. *Chance, Order, Change: The Course of International Law, General Course on Public International Law*. Leiden: Brill–Nijhoff.

Dworkin, Ronald. 1985. *A Matter of Principle*. Reprint. Cambridge, MA: Harvard University Press.

Dworkin, Ronald. 1998. *Law's Empire*. New ed. Oxford: Hart Publishing.

Fuller, Lon L. 1969. *The Morality of Law: Revised Edition*. New Haven, CT: Yale University Press.

Haas, Benjamin. 2017. "China Abandoning Rule of Law, Human Rights Lawyers Say." *Guardian*, January 24. https://www.theguardian.com/world/2017/jan/24/china-abandoning-rule-of-law-human-rights-lawyers-say.

Hart, H. L. A. 1984. *Essays in Jurisprudence and Philosophy*. Oxford: Oxford University Press.

Hayek, F. A. 1978. *Law, Legislation and Liberty*. Vol. 1, *Rules and Order*. Chicago: University of Chicago Press.

Hayek, F. A. 2007. *The Road to Serfdom: Text and Documents—The Definitive Edition (The Collected Works of F. A. Hayek)*. Chicago: University of Chicago Press. https://press.uchicago.edu/ucp/books/series/CWFAH.html

Hurd, Ian. 2015. "The International Rule of Law and the Domestic Analogy." *Global Constitutionalism* 4 (3): 365–95.

Kadi and Al Barakaat International Foundation v. Council and Commission. (CJEU 2008) ECR I-6351.

Kelsen, Hans. 1952. *Principles of International Law*. Clark, NJ: Lawbook Exchange.

Kenyon, Carleton. 1968. "Legal Lore of the Wild West: A Bibliographical Essay." *California Law Review* 56 (3): 681.

Knuchel, Sevrine. 2010. "State Immunity and the Promise of Jus Cogens." *Northwestern University Journal of International Human Rights* 9: 149.

Koskenniemi, Martti. 2011. *Politics of International Law*. Oxford: Bloomsbury Publishing.

McCorquodale, Robert. 2016. "Defining the International Rule of Law: Defying Gravity?" *International & Comparative Law Quarterly* 65 (2): 277–304.

Nardin, Terry. 1983. *Law, Morality, and the Relations of States*. Princeton, NJ: Princeton University Press.

Nardin, Terry. 2008. "Theorising the International Rule of Law." *Review of International Studies* 34 (3): 385–401.

Nardin, Terry, and Melissa Williams. 2005. *Humanitarian Intervention: NOMOS XLVII.* New York: New York University Press.

North, Douglass C., John Joseph Wallis, and Barry R. Weingast. 2013. *Violence and Social Orders: A Conceptual Framework for Interpreting Recorded Human History.* New York: Cambridge University Press.

Pattison, James. 2012. *Humanitarian Intervention and the Responsibility to Protect: Who Should Intervene?* Oxford: Oxford University Press.

Peerenboom, Randall. 2002. *China's Long March toward Rule of Law.* Cambridge, UK: Cambridge University Press.

Pils, Eva. 2017. "The Party and the Law." In *Routledge Handbook of the Chinese Communist Party,* edited by Willy Wo-Lap Lam, 248–65. Abingdon, Oxon, UK: Routledge.

Raz, Joseph. 2009. *The Authority of Law: Essays on Law and Morality.* 2nd ed. Oxford: Oxford University Press.

Tamanaha, Brian Z. 2004. *On the Rule of Law: History, Politics, Theory.* Cambridge, UK: Cambridge University Press.

Tomuschat, Christian. 1993. "Obligations Arising for States without or against Their Will." *Recueil Des Cours,* no. 241: 195–374.

Trebilcock, Michael J., and Ronald J. Daniels. 2009. *Rule of Law Reform and Development: Charting the Fragile Path of Progress.* Cheltenham: Edward Elgar.

Waldron, Jeremy. 2006. "The Rule of International Law." *Harvard Journal of Law and Public Policy* 30 (1): 15–30.

Waldron, Jeremy. 2011. "Are Sovereigns Entitled to the Benefit of the International Rule of Law?" *European Journal of International Law* 22 (2): 315–43.

Zgonec-Rozej, Miša. 2008. "Kadi & Al Barakaat v. Council of the EU & EC Commission: European Court of Justice Quashes a Council of the EU Regulation Implementing UN Security Council Resolutions." *ASIL Insights* 12 (22). https://www.asil.org/insights/volume/12/issue/22/kadi-al-barakaat-v-council-eu-ec-commission-european-court-justice.

Zhang, Qianfan. 2012. *The Constitution of China: A Contextual Analysis.* UK ed. Oxford: Hart Publishing.

4

The Compatibility of Constitutional Democracy and International Law

States must negotiate two claims of legal supremacy. The first comes from their internal legal systems. Domestic constitutions establish the primary rules of legal validity within a state's territory and authorize parliaments and courts, which have final authority in making, interpreting, and applying the law. Constitutional democracies suffuse their claims to legal supremacy with moral arguments about the legitimacy of their domestic institutions and the value of democratic self-determination. Indeed, legal supremacy can be taken as a direct implication of well-articulated defenses of national self-determination. Legal supremacy is a feature of state sovereignty. These defenses emerged in the writing of political philosophers, reflecting the sources of political obligations and reciprocity toward the members of one's state in recent decades (Miller 1997; Stilz 2009; Bellamy 2017; Moore 2001).

Yet the principle of domestic legal supremacy sits uneasily with international law's claim of legal supremacy. International law asserts authority to constrain state action, including action taken in conformity with domestic constitutional law. For many international legal scholars and practitioners, "the fact that international law is supreme vis-à-vis domestic law, at least within the international legal system, gives international law

Law Beyond the State. Carmen E. Pavel, Oxford University Press (2021). © Oxford University Press.
DOI: 10.1093/oso/9780197543894.003.0005

a constitutional-type role at the domestic level" (Dunoff and Trachtman 2009, 19–20). As the body of treaties, customs, principles, and norms that regulate relations among states, international law constrains state action for the sake of international peace or the protection of human rights. For example, the UN Charter, in force since 1945, demands that members refrain from using force in settling their disputes and from interfering in the affairs of other states (Article 2, paragraphs 2, 3, and 4), and authorizes action to ensure that nonmembers comply with its principles (Article 2, paragraph 6).[1] Domestic and international law regulate state action simultaneously, which means that states can be faced with conflicting legal obligations under the two legal systems.

The fact that national constitutions and international law put forward competing claims of legal supremacy need not necessarily be a problem. States perform many actions that are outside of the purview of international law. However, as international law steadily expands into areas previously considered the exclusive legal prerogative of sovereign states, such as import tariffs and subsidies to domestic producers, environmental protection, control over territorial waters, or the treatment of citizens and foreigners residing on their territory, the possibility of clashes between the authority of domestic and international law increases, as states' obligations under international law can come into conflict with the obligations they incur under domestic law. For example, a country can authorize via parliamentary action a war against another state in accordance with its constitutional rules, and yet the rules of the UN Charter can prohibit that war as detrimental to international peace, or as an unjustified interference with the sovereign authority of another state. The executive can demand increased tariffs on foreign imports in violation of WTO rules, which require that negotiated tariffs remain at agreed levels. And domestic courts can refuse to give effect to the decision of international courts.

This unsettled conflict between two claims of legal supremacy—domestic and international—exists for all countries, not just for constitutional democracies. But constitutional democracies raise the biggest challenge to the legal supremacy of international law, because their claims to supremacy rest on an often-unstated reliance on the moral value of democratic self-determination. Thus, compared to ordinary violations of the law represented by cases in which weak-willed or ill-meaning agents fail to fulfill their obligations, violations of international law stemming from the demands of constitutional supremacy are qualitatively different. The legal authority of various institutions in a constitutional democracy is democratically sanctioned, which comes with a special moral force and normative legitimacy. Therefore, even when these institutions make decisions which undermine international law, they are often seen as a legal and perhaps moral expression of collective self-government. Thus, one of the unappreciated features of constitutional supremacy is its democratically sanctioned potential to undermine international law and ultimately undermine the protection it affords to states and to the rights and interests of their citizens.

It is worth noting at the outset that the cases in which substantive constitutional provisions conflict directly with the provisions of international law are rare. What is far more common, however, are cases in which domestic institutions assert exclusive prerogatives to interpret states' international legal obligations and to make a final, determinative decision on a legal issue where domestic and international law overlap. The common consequence of states exercising that prerogative are decisions that states are judges in their own cases, which undermines the possibility of an international legal order. Despite the VCLT requirement that states do not interpret their domestic law so as to undermine their international legal obligations, states find justifications based in their own legal rules to openly flaunt international law and thus undermine the latter's claim to legal supremacy.

The prima facie incompatibility between constitutional democracy and international law manifests itself in several distinct ways. First, constitutional rules are potential obstacles to countries joining important international treaties. The constitution of Ireland contained provisions that precluded it from becoming a member of the Rome Statute of the ICC. The powers that were granted to the ICC had been considered the exclusive prerogative of the Irish government (DFAT 2018). Ireland resolved the incompatibility with a constitutional amendment that allowed it to ultimately join the ICC.[2]

Other countries resolve this incompatibility by registering reservations to the provisions of a treaty that come into direct conflict with their domestic laws and constitutional rules, thus making the provisions of the treaty inapplicable, as the United States did when it registered reservations to the provisions of the International Covenant for Civil and Political Rights contravening its constitutional protections for free speech (Ash 2005). The question for present purposes is not whether such reservations are justified. Some of them may be, and I believe the United States was justified to make a reservation when the protection afforded by international treaties was lower than that provided by constitutional rules. But such cases are rare. More often than not, reservations based on domestic legal provisions create bespoke exceptions from rules that should otherwise have general force, as the many reservations to the Convention on the Elimination of All Forms of Discrimination Against Women show.[3] In this context, the more important question is whether reservations weaken the ability of international rules to have wide applicability and therefore to establish norms that all states must follow, either in their treatment of their citizens or in achieving common ends.

Second, a country can choose to pass new laws or fail to repeal existing domestic laws inconsistent with the obligations stemming from treaties it has committed to. The United States has failed to repeal laws granting subsidies, preferential loans, and insurance terms to its cotton farmers which were inconsistent with WTO rules that prohibited special treatment for domestic agricultural producers, and it has also failed to review its procedural rules in order to grant rights to foreign nationals stemming from the Vienna Convention on Diplomatic Relations, as the *Brazil–US Cotton* case before the WTO and the *Avena* case before the ICJ, respectively, have shown.

Third, new governments can withdraw from treaties which previous governments have entered into, as the United States did recently in the case of the Paris Agreement or the Philippines did in the case of the ICC. These actions have stemmed from the exercise of executive power, which in many countries enjoys extensive foreign affairs prerogatives that enables it to renounce its international legal commitments or declare war on other countries in direct violation of the former's international legal obligations.

These examples show a real incompatibility between the two claims of legal supremacy, both of which enjoy normative legitimacy. Sovereign states should be entitled to make law on their territory as an expression of their sovereign autonomy. Nonetheless, domestic legal orders should not, to the extent possible, stand in the way of international legal cooperation to protect human rights, solve collective action problems such as climate change, or protect the authority of states from interference. We should thus find a way to organize the relationship between domestic and international legal orders which protects domestic law while giving support to a more robust system of international law. Changing the existing relationship is made possible by the fact that the incompatibility between their claims of legal supremacy is only a contingent feature of the relationship between the existing state-based legal rules and international law. It can be reduced or resolved by changes in rules at both the domestic and the international levels, and I will suggest a certain way of resolving it that does the least possible damage to domestic constitutional supremacy while reconciling it with some of the central demands of international law.

The first section of the chapter will explain the reasons for the legal incompatibility of the two supremacy claims by drawing on the constitutional rules of advanced democracies and on the provisions of international treaties and the UN Charter. The following sections will consider various moral and legal arguments for whether and how the incompatibility should be resolved. The second section focuses on arguments which claim that the incompatibility should not be resolved. The third will summarize and challenge some of the most common arguments for resolving the conflict in favor of domestic constitutional supremacy. The fourth will describe the alternative I defend and begin to sketch its institutional implications.

CONFLICTING CLAIMS OF LEGAL SUPREMACY

State-based legal supremacy has evolved in response to a problem fundamental for the stability of any legal system: the finality of legal judgments. In constitutional systems, finality is a solution to a number of distinct and related challenges: the stability of the rules, their determinacy, and legal coherence. The stability of the rules, and of the interpretation given to them by the law's subjects, is essential for ensuring clear, predictable behavioral guidelines that do not change too much over time or through successive governments. Change is part and parcel of any evolving legal system, but change must be managed and directed in such a way as to take place according to rules that most recognize as legitimate, and which does not radically undermine the gains in peaceful coexistence that a stable legal system makes possible. Constitutional rules are more entrenched than ordinary legislation precisely to render them more stable and require higher democratic standards of authorization.

Finality is an answer to the need for stability, but also to the indeterminacy of legal rules. Legal indeterminacy is a consequence of the generality of the law. Most actions prohibited or permitted by law are described in general terms, and it is impossible for the law to specify in advance all the circumstances to which it applies. Legal subjects resolve the indeterminacy by interpreting for themselves what the law requires, until they are challenged by others who hold conflicting interpretations of the same rules. Those challenges sometimes end up in courts, which resolve the indeterminacy by favoring a specific interpretation of a general rule. Embracing the idea that court judgments can be themselves fallible, many constitutional legal systems allow appeals and contestations of the initial court judgment. But the appeals cannot go on forever. There needs to be a stopping point at which the interpretation is settled and the matter adjudicated with finality. Appeals and constitutional courts often play the role of courts of last resort. They hold supreme authority over the lower courts to settle the issue of legal interpretation. This finality of legal judgment is not absolute. Courts can reverse their decisions, and parliaments can change the law. But while the interpretation of the law and the law itself is to some extent revisable, the interest of any legal system in finality is strong and ensures the stability of its laws over time and the predictability that enables the legal subjects to plan their lives and actions in accordance with the law.

In addition to issues of indeterminacy and stability, finality is necessary to deal with the common occurrence of conflicts of legal norms, such as those that arise in US law between religious freedom and nondiscrimination, or between groups exercising cultural rights and individual autonomy. Conflicts between legal rules create the possibility of legal incoherence, when behavior is seemingly required (or permitted) by one rule and prohibited by another. When a religious organization fires an employee for not abiding with its religious tenets, a question arises about whether it has the liberty to do so given provisions defending the free exercise of religion, which coexists with those protecting individuals against discrimination. Similarly, groups exercising the freedom to shape their cultural identity may impose restrictions on their members that run afoul of protections for individual autonomy. Both individual rights and group cultural rights may be protected by the law, and a conflict ensues about which legal norm should take priority in a given context.

Conflicts of law arise in advanced legal systems also because the latter often develop multiple lawmaking and law-adjudicating institutions. For example, federal states have state and federal parliaments, and in those with a common law history, customary norms play an important role in generating primary rules of behavior or secondary rules for making and changing the law. Legal coherence requires relatively clear orders of precedence among the pronouncements of various lawmaking authorities and among courts that interpret the law and adjudicate disputes.

Constitutional supremacy has been developed as a principle to handle internal problems of stability, indeterminacy, and incoherence at the state level, yet with the development of international law, these problems have only been replicated at the global level. For example, incoherence about what international law demands is made possible by overlapping jurisdictions of national and international legal bodies; by the relative paucity of international courts to adjudicate conflicts arising from indeterminate rules; and by the rapid change and proliferation of international treaties, which themselves can make conflicting demands on states.

Constitutional democracies maintain legal coherence in the face of proliferating international law through a variety of supremacy clauses that entrench the authority of the former over the latter. Countries such as the United States, Canada, Australia, and France grant domestic institutions authorized specifically for this purpose the power to decide the extent to which international law applies. Article VI of the US Constitution stipulates that the Constitution, the laws made by the US Congress in accordance with it, and international treaties are the law of the land. An interpretation of this clause that now prevails among judicial bodies and legal scholars is that the Constitution is supreme over international law, giving Congress, the president, and the Supreme Court the final authority to determine whether and in what manner international law is binding on US soil (Hathaway 2009; Bradley and Goldsmith 2018; Paulsen 2009; Hollis, Blakeslee, and Ederington 2005).[4]

Article 51 of the Australian constitution gives Parliament the ultimate decision-making power with respect to international law via its "external affairs" clause: "[T]he Parliament shall, subject to this Constitution, have power to make laws for the peace, order, and good government of the Commonwealth with respect to external affairs."[5] The High Court of Australia held in the case *Commonwealth v. Tasmania*, as well as in *Richardson v. Forestry Commission* and *Victoria v. Commonwealth*, that the way for the Parliament to exercise this power with respect to foreign relations is to engage in deliberate lawmaking to incorporate the obligations of the international treaty into domestic legislation.[6] The Parliament, however, can choose not to incorporate international treaties, giving them no effect or incorporating them selectively and with substantively different rules. In fact, after a review of the Senate's legal commission, the Australian government decided that it will not ratify treaties unless it decides that ratification is in the national interest.[7]

Section 52 of the Canadian constitution likewise provides that "the Constitution of Canada is the supreme law of Canada, and any law that is inconsistent with the provisions of the Constitution is, to the extent of the inconsistency, of no force or effect," and this includes contrary international law. In general, foreign treaties do not have legal effect without implementing legislation (Weiss 1998; Stephane Beaulac 2019; Stéphane Beaulac 2004).[8] According to article 53 of its constitution, France likewise requires that international treaties and agreements, "may be ratified or approved only by an Act of Parliament."[9] What the provisions in these various constitutions show is that many advanced democracies consider themselves to have final authority on whether international law has force domestically and in what manner. This means that although international law has independent authority, the language of constitutional supremacy can have the effect of rendering international law subject to the will of national bodies and legally meaningful to them to the extent that they choose. This does not mean that international law ceases to be binding on states which refuse to comply with it, but that the principle of constitutional supremacy enables various domestic institutions to vastly diminish the practical effects of international law's legal authority.

Other countries are more deferential to international law, but while they grant it legal status equal to or higher than national law, international law typically has a lower status than constitutional rules and principles. The Netherlands offers the most striking example of a constitution committed to respecting international law. Article 90 generates an obligation to "promote the development of the international legal order," while article 93 says that treaties and the resolution of international organizations become binding after publication. Moreover, article 94 provides that national laws that come into conflict with international law provisions shall not apply, thus giving international law superior status to national legislation, but not to constitutional rules.[10] The Netherland's constitutional court is only authorized to strike down national legislation inconsistent with international law, and it has otherwise no extended authority to review national legislation. In Germany, article 25 of the constitution is called "The Primacy of International Law" and provides that "the general rules of international law shall be an integral part of federal law. They shall take precedence over the laws and directly create rights and duties for the inhabitants of the federal territory."[11] While the Spanish constitution does not have such clear priority rules in its text, it states in article 96 that international treaties must be directly incorporated into domestic law upon publication.[12]

In this second group of countries, domestic incorporation of international law does not require implementing legislation, international law creates obligations and rights upon ratification, it can be used by individuals to bring claims against their states in national courts, and it is directly invoked by judges in deciding cases. By contrast, in other countries, without incorporation into domestic law, international law has little effect. It cannot be invoked by judges in their decisions, and it does not create rights for individuals or other states. An important feature of all countries' constitutional systems is that only treaties that *they choose to join* have effect; therefore there is a strong voluntarist element in their relationship to international law. No international treaty applies without a country's consent, although customary international law typically does.

The reason why this is important is that, as a matter of legal practice, national and international law can have overlapping areas of regulation, and when they come into conflict, the question arises about which of the two bodies of law—the domestic or the international—has priority in a given territory. This is especially important for rules essential for the maintenance of international peace, such as the use of force, but also many other areas such as human rights, economic, and environmental law, in which national and international rules could be at odds. In theory, and often in practice, countries can reject their obligations in international law on the basis of the authority delegated to domestic institutions. And if every country has the authority granted by its constitution to disregard international law, the latter ceases to be meaningful and authoritative.

This is because first, treaties aimed at solving collective action problems that require widespread buy-in from states cannot get off the ground when a critical mass among them holds out. Second, even when treaties do not solve collective action problems and thus could be operative without widespread buy-in, lack of support from constitutional democracies weakens their moral legitimacy and their ability to gather institutional and material support for implementation. Third, the ability of states to withhold consent, make reservations, or withdraw consent creates reasonable concerns of selective applications, hypocrisy, and discrimination for rules that should bind all, such as the rules of international criminal law. And finally, the ability to withdraw at will from or violate long-standing treaties undermines the stability of international rules and the economic and political gains they have made possible.

As a body of rules that constrain and coordinate state action, international law aspires to be authoritative and contains various provisions to cement its supremacy over national law. Indeed, the UN Charter, signed by most existing sovereign states, establishes itself at the top of the hierarchy in international law, in relation to other international law as well as national law. Article 103 states that members' obligations under the UN Charter override their obligations under any other treaty. Article 104 states that the UN shall enjoy on the territory of each member nation legal capacity as it may be necessary to fulfill its function. Moreover, the VCLT, in force since 1980 as a foundational document that establishes secondary rules in international law for the making, changing, interpreting, and terminating of treaties, contains in Article 27 the clause that "a party may not invoke the provisions of its internal law as justification for its failure to perform a treaty."[13] There is a strong conceptual necessity for this kind of clause. International law could not exist as a system if states could avoid their legal obligations by passing domestic laws contrary to it. The same could be said of domestic law, which would be rendered meaningless by individuals contracting out of it, say when spouses decide to avoid the legal obligation to pay taxes via a contract between them.

As a constitutive document of international law, the Charter does not only affirm the superiority of international legal norms but also grants coercive authority to the Security Council to enforce them. The Security Council has broad investigative powers related to any dispute between states that could cause friction and give rise to a conflict, may call on parties to settle their disputes through peaceful means, and may make any recommendations for the settlement of such disputes it deems necessary. Under Chapter VII of the Charter, the Security Council has authority to determine any threat to peace or breach of peace and take any action, including military action, "to maintain or restore international peace and security." Since the meaning of "international peace" and "security" are left intentionally broad, the Security Council has extraordinary and vast coercive powers over states. In practice, the Security Council is limited by the willingness of its permanent and nonpermanent members to cooperate, and by the willingness of the general UN base to make available military support for its operation. This de facto limitation means that it exercises its power cautiously and with difficulty. Nonetheless, the Security Council has ultimate and exclusive authority to decide when breaches of international peace are happening and to act against them. To date, it has approved numerous operations for the maintenance of peace and security with Chapter VII authorization and has interpreted its authority broadly to authorize interventions for humanitarian purposes (Lowe and Tzanakopoulos 2011).

Given the potential incompatibility that arises from claims of national constitutional supremacy and the supremacy of international law, two immediate questions arise: Should such legal incompatibility be resolved, and if so, should a solution favor constitutional supremacy over international law or vice versa? Answers to these questions typically contain a blend of political, legal, moral, and descriptive claims.

SHOULD THE INCOMPATIBILITY BE RESOLVED?

Rather than resolve the potential incompatibility of national and international law, proponents of legal pluralism embrace it as a positive way to express diverse values. Legal pluralists maintain that as a descriptive matter, international politics is governed by a plurality of legal orders, including state, regional, and international law, which overlap and interact in complex ways, without any one of them having ultimate or supreme authority in case of conflicts. But they make a further normative claim that reducing this plurality by creating clear orders of precedence between national and international law would sweep over legitimate and important social and legal differences represented by each legal system, would fail to address concerns over the quality of international law, and would undermine the possibility of states to pursue their interests as effectively as possible (Krish 2012; Berman 2007; Koskenniemi 2011). Without giving a full account of the richness of the pluralist position on embracing incompatibility, I will explain why it fails to persuade, before moving on to consider giving priority to the claims of domestic law. In the final section I will defend a particular balance between the claims of domestic and international law.

Defending a plurality of "norm-generating communities" involves denying any one of them special legitimacy or authority in making law. The creative possibilities embodied in the existence of multiple overlapping jurisdictions for solving problems would be undermined either by giving primacy to state legal systems or by proclaiming the superiority of international law (Berman 2007, 302, 307).

An important problem with legal pluralism is that it is not entirely clear what its normative commitments are. When legal pluralism is not just a descriptive claim about the world but a model for how we should organize it, we need to understand the moral reasons behind this model. One way to provide moral grounding for legal pluralism is to maintain that a plurality of values expressed in various legal orders is a good in itself. Namely, the world is better off, in some sense, if more rather than fewer values are realized across various legal communities. But there is no special reason to think that a plurality of values is intrinsically valuable apart from the benefit it brings to individuals who are subject to laws of the communities who express or embody those values. And we can more easily see that pluralism can be a problem insofar as orders within a pluralist universe can seriously harm, oppress, and commit large-scale violence against individuals. Thus, a defense of legal pluralism must be responsive to and incorporate the moral value of individuals as constraints on the permissible range of legal systems within a pluralist order. Such responsiveness can take various forms, from respecting individual rights to respecting people's capacity for collective self-determination. But what is clear is that not just any kind of pluralism will do, but one that also places limits on the capacity of various jurisdictions and communities to treat unjustly individuals or groups. A morally defensible pluralism is one that recognizes these limits.

Therefore, the main problem with unconstrained legal pluralism is that communities within a pluralist system can be internally oppressive or externally belligerent or express in their legal system values that are indefensible. States engage in widespread human rights violations of the rights of their citizens or violations of the rights of other states, and when this happens, it is not clear that legal pluralism has a good answer to how to minimize these serious problems. If pluralists recognize international rules as one category of rules among many, with no special weight or authority over states, pluralists cannot explain why states should change their behavior without recognizing some hierarchy of values, or what would be an appropriate institutional system that encourages them to do so, without giving priority to some of the rules of international law.

Moreover, legal pluralism is difficult to reconcile with a concern for legal stability and certainty. Having a plurality of state legal orders for which international rules are optional and states are judges in their own cases leads to partiality, unwieldy fragmentation, and legal chaos, or at the very least to a situation in which states continuously challenge the authority of international law and therefore the very possibility of having common rules that bind them. Without international law, states cannot achieve common ends like peace or environmental protection. Furthermore, when they contest each other's jurisdiction, they lack institutional mechanisms on the basis of which to agree on the bounds of their authority and on the demarcation of their territorial and resource rights.

The problem is not pluralism as such. Indeed, pluralism can be embraced and nurtured as long as it is constrained by general rules, and federal and multinational states often do so within the framework of a constitutional hierarchy. Thus, the contrast between pluralism and hierarchy is overdrawn. Pluralism and hierarchy can coexist in various degrees, and legal pluralism can be enhanced and preserved in constitutional orders which recognize and protect various lawmaking communities, sources, and levels. Rather, the problem with the current legal pluralism at the international level is that when the interpretations of international rules in national and international courts differ, the existing procedures for coordinating their judgments are insufficient. Also, since international rules do not define and protect just the rights of states, but also of individuals living in them, under pluralism there remains considerable uncertainty about the nature and status of those rights. Among the plural legal orders that comprise international law, some not only fail to protect individual rights but are serous violators of those rights. Such "pluralism" should not be celebrated but curtailed. As Turkuler Isiksel has shown, the unconstrained legal pluralism of the existing international system condones the domination of weak by the powerful, encourages states to ignore the negative externalities they impose on other states, and offers few constraints against states which commit persistent and widespread human rights violations (Isiksel 2013, 186–88). Thus, while acceptance of legal pluralism is inevitable as long as we recognize states' sovereignty and territorial jurisdiction, we need better tools to solve the incompatibility, at least on issues fundamental to international peace and order and the protection of individual rights.

IN FAVOR OF THE SUPREMACY OF NATIONAL CONSTITUTIONS

The issue of legal supremacy raises a distinctive philosophical problem: Who is to have the final say on the laws which govern a political community? Those who favor national constitutional supremacy do so on the grounds that it best reflects the value of democratic self-rule. It is "We the People" of each state that have historically represented the constituent power with authority to establish the law of the land and a constitution that is supreme (Kumm 2005, 274–28; Niesen 2017, 187–90; Patberg 2016, 631–33; 2018, 4–7; Bellamy 2017, 5–11). Several different strands of arguments have developed, focused on the moral value of sovereign autonomy for collective self-determination and the instrumental but essential role states play in securing the rights of their citizens. Skepticism of international law on these strands derives from a moralized account of the value of national self-creation and of the independence of states from outside interference. I will call this position the *statist constitutionalist* view. I will show that insofar as it claims the exclusive legal authority of national constitutions and domestic legal institutions over international law, it faces important limitations, which the alternative I will defend in the following section does not.

Political philosophers focus less on the interface between constitutional law and international law and more on the reasons citizens rely on to affirm the value of national institutions, including national law. Statist political theorists such as David Miller, Anna Stilz, and Margaret Moore defend the primacy of national institutions against a more cosmopolitan view of the reach of justice. I will argue that this position can be plausibly reconstructed as a statist constitutionalist position, namely one favoring the supremacy of national law over international law. David Miller claims that states are the center of a special community, the national community, which is a source of identity and particular associative obligations. The sovereign state is the vehicle which historically has allowed claims of national self-determination to be realized (Miller 1997, 10–11). Miller and Moore argue that the state allows a community who share a distinctive public culture and a territory to build institutions that express reciprocal loyalties and obligations through an evolving conception of justice (Miller 1997, 27, 67–79; Moore 2001, 28–31). The members of such communities draw on a common history and shared values to negotiate the outlines of that conception of justice, to use it as a framework for laws and policies which protect basic rights, and to assign responsibility for claims of distributive justice (Miller 1997, 79).

Anna Stilz defends the primacy of political obligations citizens have to their states, not on the ground of a national culture that is particularistic and distinct, but on the ground that states are necessary to instantiate universal liberal values. A state which deserves allegiance must promote and affirm liberal democratic values that realize the moral ideal of equal freedom for individuals. Citizens owe their states political allegiance because "only a state can create the conditions in which equal freedom between individuals is realized" (Stilz 2009, 22). One interpretation of Stilz's view is that constitutional democracies, insofar as they protect the kinds of minimal individual rights to participation and protection from interference with individual autonomy, are precisely the kinds of states that qualify for allegiance (Stilz 2009, 81–84). Constitutional democracies are morally significant for realizing an ideal of justice that could not be obtained any other way. This is why they generate special obligations for their citizens to respect their laws and give priority to the political obligations they owe to their particular states, not to other states or to global institutions.

Richard Bellamy defends the primacy of state sovereignty on the grounds of nondomination. On the republican account of nondomination, individuals as moral equals are entitled to autonomous choice, and that choice is undermined when they are subject to alien control (Bellamy 2017, 5; Pettit 1999, 73–75). Individuals can be dominated either by coercive control or simply by the threat of interfering with one's agency. Popular sovereignty embodied in state political institutions offers a solution to the problem of domination, by creating neutral, impartial, deliberative democratic decision mechanisms that enable individuals to retain considerable scope for individual autonomy and create restrictions only in the name of rules that they assent to as free and equal (Bellamy 2017, 7–8). Miller, Moore, Stilz, and Bellamy are among those who, like Yael Tamir, Will Kymlicka, and others, argue that preference for national institutions is a necessary part of realizing liberal democratic principles (Tamir 1995, 69, 101; Kymlicka 1989, 125). Obligations to respect and uphold their state's law above any other law is part of this constellation of special obligations that individuals have, along with paying taxes, contributing to the welfare of fellow citizens in a scheme of social distribution, voting, and participating in national politics. Pushed to the extreme, one implication of this view could be that allegiance to national laws and institutions must be exclusive in order for citizens to express their obligations of justice, reciprocity, and fairness to one another. On this extreme reading, allegiance to national constitution is simply not compatible with allegiance to international law (Buchanan and Powell 2008).

Importantly, none of the defenders of statist loyalty take this extreme view that allegiance to state institutions must be exclusive. Although "We the People" is fundamental, Miller and Stilz for example both acknowledge obligations of justice to outsiders. No state is a self-contained, isolated whole, and every state incurs obligations for its actions when they have detrimental effects on other states, or when it engages in joint projects with them (Miller 1997, 100–105; Stilz 2009, 168). And Bellamy insists that international rules protecting state sovereignty are necessary if states are to secure nondomination by other states, with the EU as a possible test case in this regard (Bellamy 2017, 11–13; 2014, 1032–33; Laborde and Ronzoni 2016, 281–83). Indeed, democratic procedures ensure internal sovereignty, but there must be institutional mechanisms to ensure external sovereignty, namely protections for the authority of popular sovereigns to make their own decisions without the fear of domination by outside alien forces. Protections of state sovereignty via regional or international rules can accomplish this goal (Bellamy 2017, 10–11).

Apart from Bellamy, so far political philosophers have for the most part avoided making any pronouncements on the role of constitutional supremacy in relation to international law. However, one less extreme but plausible interpretation of their view is to argue that citizens assert precisely this kind of supremacy in their constitutional document as a way of affirming the moral value of democratic self-determination against encroachment from outsiders, and therefore these views can be interpreted as a version of statist constitutionalism.

Thus, it is yet unclear whether statist constitutionalists' acceptance of moral obligations beyond borders translates into support for the authority of international law. This is because recognizing the authority of international law would require states and citizens to give primacy to some of its demands over the demands of their state institutions and laws (Pavel and Lefkowitz 2018). Statist constitutionalists could respond that domestic laws could also recognize duties to outsiders, and that this would obviate the need to accede to the supremacy of international law. But concerns of justice embodied in international law, such as human rights, international peace, or protecting the environment, depend first and foremost on international cooperation in order to be effective and require widespread coordination and a uniform understanding of states' obligations. A patchwork of domestic constitutional commitments to these values would not be sufficient. Therefore, we need a better account of the legal implications of these broader notions of responsibility that go beyond national borders in cases of conflict between a domestic constitutional order and the authority of international law.

State consent to international treaties on a case-by-case basis may be considered to preserve this kind of democratic self-determination, insofar as democracies empower representative and political officials to make decisions on their behalf in the area of foreign affairs. But state consent can be especially problematic for statist constitutionalists when the number of international treaties becomes very large, since it has the consequence of transferring substantial lawmaking power to the international level, where law that binds one's community is made by representatives of other countries who are not accountable to that community, in international processes which may lack a strong democratic pedigree. In countries such as the United States, where the doctrine of executive power in foreign affairs has meant that the president enjoys unprecedented lawmaking power when entering into executive agreements with other nations, the conditions for democratic self-determination could be further undermined. One could argue that such power is based on an outdated understanding of the proper division of authority between different spheres of government, as it was granted at a time when the founders did not anticipate the extensive role that international law would play in domestic affairs, and thus an extensive executive prerogative is no longer conducive to collective self-determination. State consent to international law could indeed undermine the conditions for democratic government, and thus calls to restrict it would be consistent with a statist constitutionalist position.

Reflecting on the purpose of international rules that limit the use of force in international affairs, as well as the principles of noninterference and equality of states, should buttress support for the supremacy of international law in certain key areas. Indeed, these principles serve the central goal of international peace, without which states cannot realize many if not most of the benefits they bestow on their citizens, including social justice and the protection of basic rights. One might go further and argue that requiring respect for rules and principles of international law is a precondition for states exercising their authority and providing public goods for their citizens, or for realizing universal liberal values. As such, respect for the authority of international law is a necessary condition of respect for the authority of state constitutions. As Allen Buchanan and Russel Powell show, at most defenders of the value of constitutional democracy can show that international law poses some risks to the former, but not that the risks are such that they warrant its outright rejection (Buchanan and Powell 2008, 329, 339–45). The implication of this understanding of the essential role international rules play in securing a safe space for states to develop their institutions is that at least on some essential issues, international law should take priority.

Statist constitutionalists would be right to insist that such a concession is contingent on the justice and democratic pedigree of international law. International law cannot enjoy authority whatever its content and whatever the process that creates it. Indeed, there are legitimate concerns about the disproportionate influence powerful nations have in the making of numerous international treaties and the lack of inclusivity of diverse voices and interests. I believe such concerns place constraints on the shape and content of instruments that would enable the primacy of international law, but they can be accommodated by a proper division of labor between national and international law, as I will show in the last section.

Therefore, statist constitutionalists need not be hostile to the proper authority of international law. In fact, nothing in their theoretical machinery prevents them from taking on board an attitude more deferential to international law, provided that such deference is strongly qualified. That is, statist constitutionalists can insist on a principle of national constitutional supremacy on many if not most issues they believe states should assert exclusive jurisdiction over, as long as they accommodate the idea that on some issues, international law must be supreme.

To sum up, the moralized account of statist constitutionalism does not offer good reasons for a wholesale rejection of the authority of international law. The more important question becomes: If states are to accept the authority of international law, what institutional form should that division of authority take, and what is the proper balance between the two spheres? The next section offers a provisional answer to this fundamental question, and the next chapter elaborates further.

IN FAVOR OF THE PARTIAL SUPREMACY OF INTERNATIONAL LAW

The main purpose of this chapter has been to diagnose the problem of the potential and contingent incompatibility between constitutional democracy and international law and argue that it is a problem in need of a solution. I can only begin to sketch the outline of that solution here and in the next chapter as an invitation to a dialogue about the range of possible responses. The first thing to note is that if constitutional supremacy is not the best solution to the incompatibility of national and international law, neither is a blanket grant of supremacy to international law. International law is a weakly institutionalized, imperfect legal order, and it raises important issues of justice and rule of law of its own. The well-known *Kadi* case before the Court of Justice of the European Union has invalidated rules stemming from the Security Council resolution creating lists of individuals and organizations accused of aiding terrorist groups, by showing that such rules violate due process and property rights. Moreover, international institutions tasked with creating, applying, and enforcing international rules are prone to well-documented pathologies and problems of legitimacy (Barnett and Finnemore 1999). But luckily, the choice is not binary: we must choose neither the exclusive supremacy of national constitutional democracy over international law, nor the exclusive supremacy of international law over national constitutional law.

The question about the proper hierarchy of norms and institutions between domestic and international law is itself a constitutional problem, in the sense that it arises out of a demand for stability, coherence, and finality of the rules of international law. The stability of international law is undermined when states fail to align their domestic legislation to their international legal obligations, rescind the authority they grant to international courts or fail to grant them authority in the first place, and when new governments renege on previous governments' international commitments for political reasons. The United States is notorious for withdrawing its consent to the jurisdiction of the ICJ in the wake of unfavorable decisions (see, e.g., *Nicaragua v. The United States of America*,

ICJ 1986, or *Avena–Mexico v. The United States of America*, ICJ 2004). When states withdraw consent to the authority of international courts, they create additional uncertainty about the seriousness of their legal commitments stemming from treaties which delegate interpretive and adjudicative power to those courts (Quigley 2009). The stability of subjects' commitment to law is one of the principal problems a constitutional order seeks to solve. It generates a binding, unwavering, constant affirmation of general secondary rules and procedures to create, change, and interpret primary rules of behavior.

In addition to its stability, international law faces challenges to its coherence. These challenges can be twofold. First, states must occasionally confront constitutional-level conflicts of legal obligations: their obligations under domestic law conflict with their obligations under international law. States can raise tariffs in accordance with their domestic constitutional procedures, and those tariffs can violate their legal obligations as members of the WTO. Technically, under the VCLT, states are not allowed to use their domestic law as a justification for violating their international legal obligations, yet due to widespread indifference to it and lack of enforcement, the VCLT rule has little effect. Second, states are subject to conflicting legal obligations from different areas of international law. The fragmentation of international law results from bodies of law which have arisen independently from each other and which have their own rules, principles, and interpretive mechanisms. For example, states' obligations under the WTO can conflict with their obligations under international environmental law. This is not a special problem of international law. Indeed, individuals can be subject to legal principles and rules which come into conflict, and when they do, domestic constitutional orders spell out mechanisms for resolving those conflicts. While international courts rely to some extent to procedural rules and interpretive maxims to attenuate these conflicts, they continue to disagree on a number of important interpretive issues (Pauwelyn 2003). For example, the International Tribunal for the Former Yugoslavia (ICTY) and the ICJ provided different pronouncements on state responsibility for the actions of irregular militias. In fact, the ICTY considered the ICJ interpretation of international law on this matter incorrect, while the ICJ argued in a subsequent decision that the ICTY understanding was unpersuasive (Dunoff and Trachtman 2009, 6–7). Appellate bodies can "correct legal errors and bring coherency" to a body of law, and international law could benefit from constitutional appellate procedures for the decisions of international courts (Dunoff and Trachtman 2009, 13).

Of special significance is the conflict between the rules protecting fundamental human rights and those protecting sovereign authority. States which commit serious and widespread violations of their citizens' rights often invoke the norms of noninterference and sovereign immunity to avoid accountability for their acts. Unless and until new international rules spell out clear exemptions to the norms protecting state sovereignty in the name of human rights, state responsibility for human rights violations will be seriously curtailed by strong assertions of sovereign immunity. Constitutional orders often do precisely this: they enumerate a list of basic rights and explain the implications of their superior status for a variety of institutional and individual practices.

Finally, international law presents a constitutional problem due to its open-ended nature and the lack of principled limits on its authority over states. As I have argued in the previous chapter, there are strong rule-of-law reasons to consider state autonomy as deserving protection under international law, and this protection can be accomplished via a legal instrument which defines and delineates the limits of the authority of international law and institutions over states.

If international law faces all these constitutional problems, could a global constitutional pact serve as a solution? I believe that it can. I can only begin to sketch a theoretical defense of global constitutionalism, without being able to address the contentious politics that might surround it and the foreseeable problems of negotiating its content or prescribing its institutional form. Therefore, what follows is not an all-things-considered defense of global constitutionalism.

A global constitutional pact could be fairly modest and thus represent a much less radical transformation of the current legal order than one might envision at first. Such a pact could simply grant constitutional status and create explicit legal hierarchy in favor of a number of existing legal rules and principles. Among these norms are the prohibition against interference in the affairs of another state; the prohibition on the use of force; the principle of sovereign equality; and jus cogens norms which protect against large-scale violations of basic human rights, such as the prohibition against genocide, war crimes, crimes against humanity, and slavery. These principles are already considered foundational for international law and order, and a constitutional agreement would cement their authority over dissenting states; create stronger, nonoptional mechanisms for interpretation, adjudication, and enforcement; and explain more clearly orders of priority among them as well, so that, for example, states could not use the principle of noninterference as a justification for avoiding accountability for vast human rights violations.

There are additional philosophical and institutional reasons to consider global constitutionalism. A global constitution could provide a more reliable self-binding mechanism for states while at the same time protecting an extensive sphere of their legal authority, by designating a limited number of substantive and procedural issues over which international law takes priority. While a global constitutional pact that includes all countries with or without their consent is only a distant possibility, a first step could be a voluntary constitutional compact among liberal democracies and other willing nations. Such a compact would bring states closer to subscribing to a fully fledged constitutional system on select issues of importance to the international community, by creating superior norms with direct effect in national jurisdictions. A freely consented, democratic constitutional compact would allow states to legitimately bind themselves to a common set of values, rules, and principles, including basic human rights values, which take priority over national law; specify the limits of the authority of international law over national law; and create institutional mechanisms for enforcing and applying the constitutional rules so created. We already have two fairly successful models for the creation of such pacts, focused on human rights, namely the European Convention on Human Rights and the American Convention on Human Rights. I will say more about the institutional specifications for a constitutional pact in the next chapter.

For now, we ought to consider several important advantages to a global constitutional solution.

First, an international constitution would preserve intact the state system and would sanction minimal interference with states' legal authority for the sake of international peace and the protection of basic human rights. Far from undermining the system of legal pluralism that characterizes international law today, an international constitution would convert it into an *ordered pluralism*, one that would place core international norms at the center of an international legal order compelling states to accept them, regardless of their internal legal systems. A constitutional order would show due deference to national projects of self-determination by limiting the authority of international law to the norms of the international constitution. States would still be bound by international treaties that they undertake voluntarily. In contrast to a view of international law that sees it as supreme in every aspect over national law, supremacy based on an international constitution would be highly circumscribed.

Second, an international constitution would eliminate a good measure of indeterminacy and uncertainty regarding states' legal obligations, by giving international courts the last resort in interpreting those obligations in accordance with international law. International courts would replace the haphazard and self-interested interpretation of states' legal obligations by their own courts and would reduce the ability of domestic institutions to reject important international commitments whenever inconvenient. This would lead to a more unified and harmonious application of international law.

Third, an international constitution would address one of the biggest problems in international politics, which is that in the absence of clear rules of conduct, states are left to resort to political means and even military action to resolve their disagreements. A constitution could bring legal determinacy and stability, and would empower forums of last resort with compulsory jurisdiction in international law, to encourage states to solve their differences peacefully.

Fourth, an international constitutional pact that would include substantive liberal democratic values and would come about through a process that is representative and inclusive would alleviate concerns about the democratic pedigree of some of the basic norms of international law, especially when such norms would be granted constitutional status over national law. Since at first only constitutional democracies would bind themselves, concerns about representation should be much alleviated. One could even envisage popular ratification in national jurisdictions for added legitimacy. Nonetheless, since constitutional documents are more often than not constraints on majoritarian decision-making for the sake of fundamental values and individual rights, the proper balance between democratic validation and legitimation through international functional coordination in the form of regular treaty making is difficult to specify in advance and will arise out of negotiated settlements among states and other subjects of international law.

A constitutional international order would require two types of changes to the existing legal order. The first would be an international constitutional pact, gradually expanded to include more democracies and other countries willing to take part in resolving the inevitable and almost universal tensions arising between national and international law in the current system. Such a pact would decide on the international norms with supremacy over national laws, including national constitutional law, and would include the protection of sovereign equality, the prohibition on the use of force, and the principle of noninterference in the internal affairs of other states, qualified by the new constitutional norms. It would also contain, among other protections for individual rights, at a minimum the emerging jus cogens norms prohibiting genocide, crimes against humanity, slavery, and other emerging norms of the greatest concern to humanity, and provisions for the realization of collective goods such as the protection of the environment.

The second change required by a global constitutional order would be amendments to national constitutions to recognize and accept the supremacy of international constitutional norms. The many examples of constitutional changes at the national level in response to the creation of a quasi-constitutional European order, and in response to the creation of international institutions such as the ICC, are proof that such amendments are more feasible than imagined.

Neither of these changes is easy or straightforward. It is safe to say that many countries are not inclined to look favorably on the prospect of an international constitution that reduces their autonomy further, and even if they were, negotiating the content of international constitutional rules is bound to be a difficult, prolonged process. Furthermore, changes to national constitutions are difficult by design, and there will be resistance to the idea of giving up decision-making power to international institutions, be they constitutional assemblies or courts with compulsory jurisdiction. But these changes are necessary to resolve the ongoing and problematic incompatibility between the two claims of legal supremacy advanced by constitutional democracy and international law.

REFERENCES

Ash, Kristina. 2005. "U.S. Reservations to the International Covenant on Civil and Political Rights: Credibility Maximization and Global Influence." *Northwestern Journal of International Human Rights* 3 (1).

Avena and Other Mexican Nationals, Mexico v United States, ICGJ 8 (ICJ 2004).

Barnett, Michael N., and Martha Finnemore. 1999. "The Politics, Power, and Pathologies of International Organizations." *International Organization* 53 (04): 699–732.

Beaulac, Stéphane. 2004. "National Application of International Law: The Statutory Interpretation Perspective." *Canadian Yearbook of International Law/Annuaire Canadien de Droit International* 41: 225–69.

Beaulac, Stéphane. 2019. "Canada—Thinking Outside the Dualist Box? Surely Not Yet!" In *Duelling for Supremacy: International Law vs. National Fundamental Principles*, edited by Fulvio Maria Palombino, 21–42. Cambridge, UK: Cambridge University Press.

Bellamy, Richard. 2014. "The Democratic Legitimacy of International Human Rights Conventions: Political Constitutionalism and the European Convention on Human Rights." *European Journal of International Law* 25 (4): 1019–42.

Bellamy, Richard. 2017. "A European Republic of Sovereign States: Sovereignty, Republicanism and the European Union." *European Journal of Political Theory* 16 (2): 188–209.

Berman, Paul. 2007. "A Pluralist Approach to International Law." *Yale Journal of International Law* 32 (2). http://digitalcommons.law.yale.edu/yjil/vol32/iss2/3.

Bradley, Curtis A., and Jack L Goldsmith. 2018. "Presidential Control over International Law." *Harvard Law Review* 131: 1201–97.

Brazil v. The United States Upland Cotton, WT/DS267/AB/R (2005).

Buchanan, Allen, and Russell Powell. 2008. "Survey Article: Constitutional Democracy and the Rule of International Law: Are They Compatible?" *Journal of Political Philosophy* 16 (3): 326–49.

Commonwealth v. Tasmania, [1983] HCA 21.

Department of Foreign Affairs, DFAT. 2018 "International Criminal Court." Ireland's Department of Foreign Affairs and Trade. Accessed June 26, 2018. https://www.dfa.ie/our-role-policies/international-priorities/international-law/courts-tribunals-dispute-mechanisms/international-criminal-court/.

Dunoff, Jeffrey L., and Joel P. Trachtman, eds. 2009. *Ruling the World? Constitutionalism, International Law, and Global Governance*. Cambridge: Cambridge University Press.

Hathaway, Oona. 2009. "Presidential Power over International Law: Restoring the Balance." *Yale Law Journal* 119 (2): 140–383.

Hollis, Duncan B., Merritt R. Blakeslee, and L. Benjamin Ederington, eds. 2005. *National Treaty Law and Practice: Dedicated to the Memory of Monroe Leigh*. Leiden: Martinus Nijhoff.

Isiksel, Turkuler. 2013. "Global Legal Pluralism as Fact and Norm." *Global Constitutionalism* 2 (2): 160–95.

Kadi and Al Barakaat International Foundation v. Council and Commission. (CJEU 2008) ECR I-6351.

Koskenniemi, Martti. 2011. *Politics of International Law*. Oxford: Bloomsbury Publishing.

Krish, Nico. 2012. *Beyond Constitutionalism: The Pluralist Structure of Postnational Law*. Oxford: Oxford University Press.

Kumm, Mattias. 2005. "The Jurisprudence of Constitutional Conflict: Constitutional Supremacy in Europe before and after the Constitutional Treaty." *European Law Journal* 11 (3): 262–307.

Kymlicka, Will. 1989. *Liberalism, Community, and Culture*. Oxford: Clarendon Press.

Laborde, Cécile, and Miriam Ronzoni. 2016. "What Is a Free State? Republican Internationalism and Globalisation." *Political Studies* 64 (2): 279–96.

Lowe, Vaughan, and Antonios Tzanakopoulos. 2011. "Humanitarian Intervention." In *Max Planck Encyclopedia of Public International Law*. Oxford: Oxford University Press. http://opil.ouplaw.com/view/10.1093/law:epil/9780199231690/law-9780199231690-e306.

Meierhenrich, Jens, and Keiko Ko. 2009. "How Do States Join the International Criminal Court? The Implementation of the Rome Statute in Japan." *Journal of International Criminal Justice* 7 (2): 233–56.

Miller, David. 1997. *On Nationality*. Oxford: Oxford University Press.

Moore, Margaret. 2001. *The Ethics of Nationalism*. Oxford: Oxford University Press.

Nicaragua v. United States, ICGJ 112 (ICJ 1986).

Niesen, Peter. 2017. "The 'Mixed' Constituent Legitimacy of the European Federation." *JCMS: Journal of Common Market Studies* 55 (2): 183–92.

Patberg, Markus. 2016. "Against Democratic Intergovernmentalism: The Case for a Theory of Constituent Power in the Global Realm." *International Journal of Constitutional Law* 14 (3): 622–38.

Patberg, Markus. 2018. "A Systematic Justification for the EU's Pouvoir Constituant Mixte: Principles of Constitutional Politics in Supranational Polities." *European Law Journal* 23 (6): 441–53.

Paulsen, Michael Stokes. 2009. "The Constitutional Power to Interpret International Law." *Yale Law Journal* 118 (8): 1762–1842.

Pauwelyn, Joost. 2003. *Conflict of Norms in Public International Law: How WTO Law Relates to Other Rules of International Law.* New York: Cambridge University Press.

Pavel, Carmen E., and David Lefkowitz. 2018. "Skeptical Challenges to International Law." *Philosophy Compass* 13 (8): 1–14.

Pettit, Philip. 1999. *Republicanism: A Theory of Freedom and Government.* Oxford: Oxford University Press.

Quigley, John. 2009. "The United States' Withdrawal from International Court of Justice Jurisdiction in Consular Cases: Reasons and Consequences." *Duke Journal of Comparative & International Law* 19 (2): 263–306.

Richardson v. Forestry Commission—[1988] HCA 10.

Roth, Kenneth. 2000. "The Charade of US Ratification of International Human Rights Treaties." *Chicago Journal of International Law* 1: 347.

Stilz, Anna. 2009. *Liberal Loyalty: Freedom, Obligation, and the State.* Princeton, NJ: Princeton University Press.

Tamir, Yael. 1995. *Liberal Nationalism.* Princeton, NJ: Princeton University Press.

Victoria v. Commonwealth—[1996] HCA 56.

Weiss, Marley S. 1998. "Proceedings of the Seminar on International Treaties and Constitutional Systems of the United States, Mexico and Canada: Laboring in the Shadow of Regional Integration." *Maryland Journal of International Law and Trade* 22: 185.

5

Constitutionalism and Pluralism

Two Models of International Law

The legalization of international politics has moved states in incremental and uneven steps from the sphere of violent conflict, prejudice, and domination toward a rule-based order. Yet international law suffers from important structural defects, and it is worth thinking about what possible reforms can alleviate or eliminate them. I have identified some of these structural defects in previous chapters. First, proposals for reform must lessen the conflict between the legal claims of supremacy of domestic and international law, which brings legal uncertainty and weakens the possibility of rule-governed interaction among states. Second and related, states must develop better precommitment mechanisms to international law as a project which increases order, facilitates cooperation, and protects justice by continuing to embed its non-consensual elements. The strong consensual nature of international law means that states can withdraw from important international commitments at any time or register reservations to the provisions of existing treaties, thus undermining the effectiveness and legitimacy of international law. Third, rule-of-law protections for weaker states and individuals require better access to courts and enforcement mechanisms which hold powerful states accountable for violations of international law. Fourth, certain basic human rights norms must be entrenched further as checks on arbitrary, absolute state power, such that

Law Beyond the State. Carmen E. Pavel, Oxford University Press (2021). © Oxford University Press.
DOI: 10.1093/oso/9780197543894.003.0006

states' abilities to inflict large-scale harms against their citizens are limited further.

The rudiments of a solution are already present in international law as it operates today. International law contains some rules and principles with quasi-constitutional status, such as the prohibition on the use of violence, the principles of state equality and noninterference, jus cogens norms such as the prohibition against genocide, and secondary rules for the validity of treaties codified by the VCLT. The UN Charter also states in Article 2, paragraph 6 that the United Nations shall ensure that nonmembers act in accordance with its principles in order to ensure international peace. Thus, international law already contains rules which restrict the consensual character of treaty-based law, in recognition of the fact that no legal system can operate on a purely voluntary basis. Article 103 of the Charter also asserts the supremacy of Charter rules over contrary international law. But the status of all these quasi-constitutional rules is contested; they are ambiguously defined in international treaties, when they are defined at all; and the mechanisms for their interpretation and application are weak or nonexistent.[1] These principles would be better institutionalized through a constitutional pact which strengthens states' resolve to uphold them as the building blocks of an international legal order and enables more effective mechanisms for their interpretation and application.

A long list of reasons favors a constitutional solution. First, a global constitution could serve as a precommitment mechanism for states by limiting opting out from rules essential for peace, the protection of human rights, and the resolution of collective action problems. Second, a global constitutional pact could resolve conflicts of jurisdiction between states and international law and create the coherence, stability, and determinacy necessary for international law to perform its role properly. Third, a constitutional pact could create the institutional structure to facilitate the realization of global public goods. Fourth, constitutionalism is intimately bound up with the rule-of-law ideal and could strengthen the internal morality of international law, including equality before the law and access to courts. Finally, an international constitution would circumscribe the authority of international law with respect to states and individuals.

Conceived in this vein, constitutionalism increases legalization, creates direct effects for certain minimal rules of international law, and brings about the possibility of judicial review. Fundamentally, its purpose is to fortify the protections of the rights of states and individuals, to limit the arbitrary, unchecked power of international institutions over state and of states over each other and their citizens.

Thus, constitutionalism takes legalization a step further, by ensuring the internal morality of international law through rule-of-law constraints and by increasing the degree of stability, regularity, and uniformity of rules, and peaceful resolution of conflicts. It offers a new structural vision of international law by deepening the commitment to the basic values of the international community, limiting the use of public power in accordance with just principles, and ensuring its processes fulfill minimal standards of inclusivity. The constitutionalism defended here is minimalist, in the sense of containing a small set of important rules such as the regulation of the use of violence by states and other actors; protections for individuals against the worst form of abuses; and the creation or strengthening of institutions for holding perpetrators accountable, for judicial review, and for the cooperative pursuit of common goals and the resolution of collective action problems. Most other areas of international regulations would fall outside of the constitutional pact and would continue to be governed by the norms of consensual, voluntary participation of states in international agreements. Even if constitutionalism of this sort represents an ambitious plan of reform of the international legal order, substantively it is limited to a number of key areas of international regulation and cooperation. It is meant to provide a revised legal framework for international cooperation by bringing state interaction further under the sphere of law and out of the sphere of politics and diplomacy, with their attendant pathologies of violence, domination, and inequalities of power.

Attention to the constitutional character of international law is increasing (Klabbers, Peters, and Ulfstein 2009; Dunoff and Trachtman 2009a; Suami et al. 2018; Hurd 2015; Cohen 2012; Isiksel 2016). However, a significant part of this discourse embraces the language of constitutionalism not as standard for institutional reform, but as a descriptive tool to test how far one can interpret international law as a coherent legal order (Kumm 2005, 259; Dunoff and Trachtman 2009b). In fact, some scholars simply equate constitutionalization with the legalization of international politics, that is, the increased willingness of states to engage in rule-governed interaction through international treaties and customary law. However, legalization offers neither an adequate conceptual framework for understanding constitutionalism nor a blueprint for structural reform in international law. Like Nico Krish, I am interested in normatively rich conceptions of constitutionalism, which can guide political and legal reform (2012, 39).[2] Unlike him, I find that we have sufficiently robust models from domestic constitutional law for how to refashion the international legal order along constitutional lines (Dunoff and Trachtman 2009a). Substantively, constitutions articulate and protect fundamental rights, define the prerogatives of various political institutions in the system, and place explicit limitations on their power. Successful domestic constitutional systems embed the supremacy of constitutional rules via direct effect and judicial review. This means that individual rights have immediate effect on all levels of society and domains of government action, and new and old legislation must conform to them. Constitutions have thus mainly a power-defining and constraining function and a rights-defining and protecting function, and these functions are interdependent. It is because the rights defined and protected by constitutions are of fundamental importance that the exercise of political power must be carefully defined and limited through the separation of powers, the independence of the judiciary, and opportunities for contestation and redress for the law's subjects.

One of the most important challenges to constitutionalism as a normative ideal and blueprint for structural reform in international law comes from legal pluralism. Legal pluralism recognizes the inherent plurality of legal orders with claims to authority which coexist in international law and "embrace the creative possibilities inherent in multiple overlapping jurisdictions" (P. Berman 2007, 308; P. S. Berman 2006; Krish 2012; Kumm 2005). Legal pluralism consists of a descriptive and normative view. The descriptive view represents the international realm as a contest of overlapping legal systems, including state, regional, and international law, without any one of them having supremacy in cases of conflict. The normative view portrays efforts to tame legal pluralism within the constraints of a constitutional order as doing injustice "to legitimate political and social differences between states and communities within states" (Nollkaemper 2013, 98). According to this view, conflict among the claims of various communities is unavoidable in a world marked by legal pluralism, but it is also desirable insofar as it preserves the values inherent in various legal systems and avoids stifling moral, social, and legal diversity through the imposition of narrow hierarchies. I will first provide an overview of legal pluralism and then show that, despite its appeal, it has significant disadvantages as a normative ideal of international law. My concerns stem from pluralists' comfort with legal uncertainty and indeterminacy, a lack of commitment from states for a rule-based order at the international level, and the unfettered authority of deeply oppressive and unjust state legal orders over their citizens. Next, I will defend the advantages of a constitutional hierarchy over legal pluralism. Importantly, I show that constitutionalism can preserve to a large extent the pluralism inherent in international law but diminishes (without eliminating) its most important failings. Finally, I will explain why, contra existing claims to the contrary, the UN Charter does not meet the standards of an adequate constitutional treaty for international law.

LEGAL PLURALISM

Legal pluralism is difficult to pin down precisely, due to the diverse legal realities it is meant to capture. On a narrow and more defensible reading, legal pluralism refers to a context in which *various legal orders exercise overlapping jurisdiction*, such that an act may be regulated by the laws of different legal systems, and those laws could yield different, even conflicting legal requirements. Colonial legal orders were often superimposed on preexisting domestic orders and allowed the latter to function in parallel to some extent. The Austrian and Ottoman Empires had this feature, as did the various British colonies. Some modern states are also marked by legal pluralism; indigenous law, state and federal law, and the law of various cultural and religious communities (Sharia, Jewish law) operate on the same territory and claim simultaneous authority over groups of legal subjects. Thus, in the United States or Canada, an individual could be subject to indigenous law or religious law, but also to state and federal law simultaneously. Both countries settle via constitutional principles and through courts the manner in which conflicts between legal orders are handled. Therefore, these legal systems are best described as forms of pluralism limited and structured by constitutional orders. But this is not the case in the international realm, where international law coexists with the law of various states, with that of the EU and of various regional human rights and trade-based legal orders (NAFTA, the African Charter of Human and People's Rights), without any one legal system taking priority. Legal pluralism at the international level is best captured by Nico Krish:

> Pluralism eschews the hope of building one common, overarching legal framework that would integrate postnational governance, distribute powers, and provide for means of solving disputes between the various layers of law and politics. It is based instead on the heterarchical interplay of these layers according to rules ultimately set by each layer for itself. In pluralism, there is no common legal point of reference to appeal to for resolving disagreement; conflicts are solved through convergence, mutual accommodation—or not at all. It is a vision that takes societal fragmentation to the institutional level. (Krish 2012, 69)

Many international lawyers would take issue with the claim that international law is fragmented in the way described above. Indeed, they proclaim the legal supremacy of international law as a sine qua non condition of its existence. For example, Gerald Fitzmaurice wrote that the principle of supremacy is "one of the great principles of international law, informing the whole system and applying to every branch of it" (Fitzmaurice 1957, 85).[3]

This is indeed a widely shared view among international lawyers, since Dunoff and Trackmann refer to the supremacy of international law vis-à-vis domestic law as "a fact," which gives international law "a constitutional-type role at the domestic level" (2009a, 20). Equally, however, domestic constitutional orders affirm the supremacy of domestic constitutions over international law (see chapter 4), which results in incompatible claims of legal supremacy put forward simultaneously by domestic and international legal orders. These conflicting claims merely underscore the uncertainty governing the relationship between national and international law. Thus, under the present system, I view a description of the international legal order marked by legal pluralism as more apt, compared to a monist one in which there is widespread acceptance of a legal hierarchy which gives international law supremacy.

Yet besides the narrow *pluralism of legal orders*, legal pluralists sometimes refer to a broader, and much less precise, category of *pluralism of normative orders*. Drawing on Robert Cover, Paul Schiff Berman articulates legal pluralism as "constantly constructed through the contest among various norm generating communities. Thus, although 'official' norms articulated by sovereign entities obviously count as 'law,' to Cover such official assertions of prescriptive or adjudicatory jurisdiction are only some of the many ways in which normative commitments arise" (P. Berman 2007, 302; Cover 1983, 1984). According to Berman, we exist within plural, overlapping normative commitments, and preserving this plurality "create(s) openings for contestation, resistance, and creative adaptation" (2006, 1159).

This type of pluralism aims to capture a broader range of norm-generating sources, but in doing so it becomes so inclusive that it loses its relevance to questions about the proper relationship of *legal* orders. Any and all norms and norm-generating communities are potentially included in this version of legal pluralism. Consider the following norm-generating communities: football clubs, book clubs, boy and girl scouts, churches, bowling leagues, businesses partnerships, business associations, and soup kitchens. These normative communities are typically not generating legal rules, except in the context of legal contracts they enter into. Moreover, there are lots of norms that are adopted widely and shared without there being a specific community which has generated them: norms about tooth-brushing, norms limiting computer use by children, and norms requiring opening the doors for the elderly. It would be difficult to see how any of these norms are laws, and we would make a category mistake to say that they are.[4] Thus we must keep the distinction between, on the one hand, normative communities, which include the rules of football clubs, and on the other hand legal orders, which contain special types of normative rules, which are often mandatory, backed by force, meant to apply to everyone in a particular community, and attach to institutionally differentiated mechanisms for interpretation, application, and enforcement (Hart 2012; Lefkowitz 2017; C. E. Pavel 2018).

The impulse to expand legal pluralism to normative orders more generally could be simply the result of a laudable attempt to open the space of law to nonformal, alternative modes of lawmaking, from tribal and customary to hybrid, private, cultural, and religious law. That lawmaking is not comprehensively captured by the official legal pronouncements of a modern state is a valuable correction to overly formal conceptions of law tied to centralized lawmaking. In drawing attention to different sources and forms of law, pluralists point to the difficulty of delineating precisely the boundaries of law and of legal orders. Furthermore, they highlight the extent to which formal, state-based legal orders often try to replace, and thus undermine, tried and tested methods of community dispute resolution. More traditional, informal, custom-based law is often responsive to the local values and dynamics, rests on histories of rule-making fitted to the local culture, and represents repositories of local knowledge which cannot be reproduced by an impersonal state machinery. Thus, legal pluralism valorizess the hybridity of legal customs, dispute-resolution mechanisms, modes of jurisdiction, and sources of lawmaking. This hybridity is often unbound, such that it is difficult to distinguish law from other types of social rules which guide behavior.

But from the fact that it is sometimes difficult to specify precisely what types of rule-making count as law, it does not follow that we should baptize every moral, social, and religious norm with the label of law. If we did, there would be no point to calling this kind of pluralism "legal" as opposed to 'cultural" or "normative."[5] Furthermore, if we accept this much more capacious understanding of legal pluralism, in which any kind of norm counts as law, then we diminish our capacity to understand how legal rules and systems operate and interact with each other and the distinctive problems law raises for social order.[6]

Yet even if we embraced the narrower concept of legal pluralism, namely the pluralism of overlapping legal jurisdictions, several questions remain about its normative vision, namely that we should preserve and celebrate the idea that various legal orders interact with no formal structure imposed on the procedures or substantive rules of interaction. For instance, Berman insists that "of course, one thing that a pluralist approach will *not* do is provide an authoritative metric for determining which norms should prevail in this messy hybrid world. Nor does it answer the question of who gets to decide" (2006, 1165). And further: "There is no external position from which one could make a definitive statement as to who is authorized to make decisions in any given case" (P. S. Berman 2006, 1166). One would be forgiven for thinking that pluralists simply stick to a neutral description of the facts, in which they refuse to take a stand on any of the moral and legal questions that arise when legal systems come into conflict. But they do not. They claim that pluralism is itself a good worth preserving. Indeed, they believe in the "independent value of pluralism" (P. S. Berman 2006, 1167). By maintaining "equidistance to conflicting claims to ultimate authority," pluralism retains "significant strengths in providing adaptability, creating space for contestation, and offering a possibility of steering between conflicting supremacy claims of different polity levels" (Krish 2012, 70). Under pluralism "social and political relations are much more in flux, ideas about political justice are constantly shifting, and our imagination of what governance arrangements may be feasible keeps changing" (Krish 2012, 79). Based on ideas of mutual constitutional toleration developed in the context of the EU, pluralists demand that international law should allow for and encourage the mutual toleration of supremacy claims of various legal orders (Kumm 2005; Weiler 2003).

This vision opens pluralists to several challenges, none of which they can answer adequately. First, it is somewhat puzzling that pluralists defend the contemporary mode of overlapping jurisdiction at the international level, as opposed to a pluralism of, say, no international law. Pluralism has taken many different forms in different historical and geographical contexts, so unless they want to avoid the charge that they endorse whichever kind of legal pluralism happens to be in place at the particular historical time of their writing, pluralists must distinguish more carefully between qualitatively different pluralist legal structures. Otherwise, to defend a pluralism of overlapping jurisdictions consisting of state, regional, and international law means making peace with legal orders that have to a significant extent eliminated a large measure of pluralism internally, through constitutionalization, and externally, through integration via bilateral and multilateral treaties and the creation of international organizations with significant powers to interpret and apply them. Hence, states claim the supremacy of national law over competing subnational, indigenous, and other kinds of law operating on their territory. EU law claims supremacy over member states' law, which for the most part they accept. Therefore, it is difficult to see what makes the particular version of pluralism existing at the beginning of the twenty-first century more defensible than the legal pluralism present at the beginning of the twentieth century or indeed the seventeenth century.

Second, its defenders fail to offer reasons why legal pluralism is valuable and worth preserving. Without a moral defense of legal pluralism, it seems they rely on its assumed universal appeal or "independent moral value," as Berman explains. But why does pluralism have more independent moral value than its alternatives? Such a claim must be explicated and defended, and a proper defense must explain either its instrumental contribution to human well-being, liberty, and peace or its intrinsic goodness. Moral pluralism may offer important resources in this regard, although it faces philosophical challenges of its own (Crowder 2004; Kekes 1996; Chang 1998; Larmore 1987). But is it difficult to see how legal pluralism could be such a valuable human good that it is never OK to constrain it for the sake of other important goods we value, such as order, equality, liberty, or individual rights. One can easily point out that many of the communities that pluralists are keen to celebrate as part of the hybridity and multiplicity of legal orders at the international level have created and entrenched systems of oppression, abuse, and violations of rights (Stewart and Kiyani 2017). Equidistance in this international reality is morally relativist to the core, because it dignifies all existing regimes and international law with equal moral worth. Such equidistance is not desirable when it involves the values and practices of autocracies or nations who commit massive wrongs at home and abroad. There is no reason to preserve a plurality that includes those legal orders and every reason to limit the damage they can do to their subjects and to outsiders. To defend the priority of some of the rules of international law which impose legal and moral standards on all states and create avenues of accountability means precisely to limit (not eliminate) legal pluralism and to constrain regimes which fail to provide minimal protections for their subjects.

Denying the existence of an outside moral perspective useful for evaluating and indeed criticizing legal pluralism is conceivable only if one takes one of two paths. The first path is moral relativism, but the catch of moral relativism is that one has no resources to insist on the special, "independent" value of legal pluralism, because no general moral justification can be offered for preferring one institutional system over another under a relativist moral framework. Moral relativists insist on the validity of local cultural frames of evaluation and resist the acceptability of universal moral standards. No universal moral perspective is then available to defend global legal pluralism as opposed to any other structural arrangement for international law. The second path available to legal pluralists is to refuse to engage in moral philosophical evaluation tout court, and this fits with the way in which most legal scholars see their work: as mainly descriptive, interpretive, and conceptual, thus eschewing engagement with moral and philosophical analysis (Ratner and Slaughter 2004; Ratner 2013, 2019). It seems that pluralists want to go the latter route, but they cannot avoid this type of evaluation when taking the normative position they do. Legal pluralism without moral foundations cannot offer an adequate justification for preferring legal pluralism to any other structural alternative for international law, including global constitutionalism.

Third, pluralism does not offer a solution to the existential problem of international law, which is that when every state is a judge in its own case and is left to interpret its international obligations in national courts, international law is much less meaningful and authoritative. Just as domestic law cannot be left to each individual to interpret, apply, and adjudicate, so too international law needs effective, impartial mechanisms of interpretation, application, and adjudication which prevail over states. In the absence of such mechanisms, international law operates as a system of social morality more akin to norms of politeness among individuals than to law, making its rules desirable but optional. Without a coordinated, reciprocal commitment from states to give basic international rules priority over their domestic legal systems, international law cannot ensure important rule-of-law values such as regularity, predictability, due process, and the protection of human rights.

Finally, and related, pluralism fails to offer precommitment mechanisms for countries which enable them to solve collection action problems. Secondary rules for making rules are the stuff of constitutional commitments, which is why institutionalized mechanisms which spell out principles and rules for managing commons, such as representative states' assemblies, with inclusive decision procedures, are needed. What pluralism offers instead is mutual toleration, but the idea that collective action problems can be solved by mutual tolerance is at best naive, and at worst dangerous. It is naive because mutual toleration is a negative virtue which implies forbearance and perhaps respect for one another's values, but it demands no commitment to solve common problems. It is dangerous because it leaves too many individuals vulnerable to the negative externalities and injustices resulting from the actions of states and other agents and to large-scale damage resulting from climate change or the depletion of ocean resources on which many coastal communities depend for immediate survival.

Additionally, the EU's system of mutual toleration is not the right model for a pluralist international law for a number of reasons. "Mutual toleration" misdescribes a legal system in which the Court of Justice of the European Union has asserted legal supremacy and direct effect of EU law over member states, assertions to which member states have for the most part acquiesced. Second, the shared liberal constitutional consensus among member states in Europe based on strong support for democratic decision-making and the protection of individual rights makes clashes between them and the legal rules of the EU less likely (Kumm 2005, 292). This is very much not the case for international law, due to the varied degrees to which state legal systems entrench values and practices antithetical to international human rights law. And last, the political pressure to ensure consensus and the coherence of the European legal order is strong (Kumm 2005, 293), a feature again lacking in international law.

Legal pluralism at the international level ends up being deeply complacent by favoring the status quo, which is rife with problems of domination by powerful states of weak states, legal uncertainty, and human rights violations. As Martti Koskenniemi has put it, pluralism "ceases to pose demands on the world" (2007, 16).

CONSTITUTIONALIZING INTERNATIONAL LAW

Once we understand the philosophical and normative challenges of legal pluralism, we ought to be more interested in exploring constitutionalism's answer to international law's structural problems. Although in practice constitutions have various components, three are common to most written constitutional agreements. These components are *mutually interdependent and jointly necessary*: (1) substantive rules, (2) procedures or second order rules for solving collective action problems, and (3) institutional mechanisms such as courts for interpreting constitutional provisions. I will first explain why, in order to be properly constitutional, an international treaty must be *explicitly* constitutional, and then I will turn to each of these components.

To be properly constitutional, the international legal system must contain a document such as a treaty called a "constitution," which codifies constitutional rules and enables institutional mechanisms for their interpretation and application. This is not an obvious point, since some domestic legal orders are said to have "tacit" or "unwritten" constitutions. Nonetheless, creating an international constitution via a written agreement which *declares it to be a constitution* is important for symbolic, expressive, and practical reasons. This is because, first, a constitutional treaty expresses most clearly and forcefully states' precommitment to a rule-based international order; isolates precisely the norms which are subject to constitutional consensus; and requires states to go through the process of negotiating, compromising, and internalizing them. Many agreements, from marriages to contracts, accomplish this function of articulating the specifics of the commitment of the parties and cementing it only when they are explicitly discussed and negotiated and officially sanctioned. Charles Lipson explained the role formal treaties play in conveying credible commitment:

> The decision to encode a bargain in treaty form is primarily a decision to highlight the importance of the agreement and, even more, to underscore the durability and significance of the underlying promises. . . . The more formal and public the agreement, the higher the reputational costs of noncompliance. . . . States deliberately choose to impose these costs on themselves in order to benefit from the counter promises (or actions) of others. (Lipson 1991, 508–12)

A constitutional treaty will have higher status and visibility than regular treaties and can thus be expected to amplify and secure states' commitment to regular treaties. Second, just like a marriage changes the legal status of the parties and their legal obligations compared to, say, an informal domestic partnership, so too a written constitution changes the legal status of states and of the rules, procedures, and institutions embodied in it. States' rights will be better protected and their obligations more clearly articulated when states explicitly and publicly commit to a system of reciprocal, uniform constitutional constraints and institutional mechanisms created for this purpose. Moreover, an international constitution would give hierarchically superior legal status to a set of norms, procedures, and institutions, and would require that the rest of international and state law be consistent with it. Finally, a constitutional treaty must be an explicit distillation of the terms negotiated and agreed to by states to allow its language to serve as a fundamental reference point for interpreting rules and settling disagreements on constitutional essentials. As Bardo Fassbender puts it, "[I]t is one of the main purposes of a written constitution to ensure a higher degree of certainty within the law than that prevailing in a system of customary rules" (1998, 599). A written constitution thus accomplishes coordination around detailed secondary rules across the vast international community of states, individuals, international organizations, and other agents operating in the international realm.

Substantively, I defend a minimal but normatively demanding form of global constitutionalism, in the sense that it requires a progressive, incremental-step change from the current structure of international law, and it builds on the quasi-constitutional features already present in the international legal system. Among these quasi-constitutional features are jus cogens norms that prohibit the most serious breaches of human rights such as genocides, crimes against humanity, and slavery, and vital international law principles such as sovereign equality, noninterference in the internal affairs of states, and those regarding the appropriate use of force by states. The set of substantive rules can be expanded by states, but at a minimum, it would spell out more clearly limits on sovereign autonomy in the name of individual and group rights. In addition to articulating and enumerating jus cogens norms as the most plausible candidates for those limits, the constitution would define the permissible ways in which the international community can enforce them, say via humanitarian intervention and nonoptional international criminal accountability (C. Pavel 2015; Kadelbach 2006; Thouvenin 2005; Criddle and Fox-Decent 2009; Altman and Wellman 2004; Deitelhoff 2009). They will also include a new articulation and defense of sovereign autonomy, by defining domains of protection for states in which they are entitled to make their own decisions without interference from other states or the international community as a whole. Thus, a constitution would have to spell out more precisely what rights the principle of noninterference within the sovereign authority of states invoked by the UN Charter entails for states. A constitution would reiterate the limitations on the use of force by states contained in the UN Charter, which currently only allows defensive military action in response to actual attacks and outlaws all offensive military action (S. R. Ratner 2015).

An international constitution must also create second-order rules which guide the formation of international law in general and institutional mechanisms for the resolution of collective action problems more specifically. International law already contains well-developed second-order rules for the creation, validity, and termination of treaties codified in the VCLT, but these rules are beset by various important difficulties and ambiguities, such as the content of the jus cogens rules capable of restraining the capacity of states to enter into treaties; lack of clarity regarding the permissibility of reservations; and last but not least, the lack of a binding mechanism of interpretation of the VCLT rules (Pellet 2013; Djeffal 2013). A suitably revised and selective set of rules from the VCLT could be part of a constitutional agreement. Also included would be other mechanisms for addressing collective action problems, such as global warming or the management of global water commons and underwater resources, which are at present insufficiently addressed. These would take the form of procedures, fora, assemblies, and other conceivable decision-making bodies. "Enabling constitutionalism" is a well-understood if underappreciated feature of constitutional orders, in addition to constraining constitutionalism (Dunoff and Trachtman 2009b, 10–11; Isiksel 2016). Constitutional rules endow international bodies with the power to create ordinary rules. They enable the allocation of law-making authority and can specify just procedures for making decisions without committing to what those decisions should be. Such bodies and procedures must be inclusive and weigh the interests of parties variously situated with respect to these problems fairly. While imagining how to solve problems of inclusive representation on a global scale is a tall order, there is no shortage of models, from geographic and state-based representation, to lotteries, descriptive, and interest-based representation (Dovi 2002; Kuper 2004; Mansbridge 2003; T. Macdonald 2008; Dovi 2002; Rehfeld 2005; Stone 2011). Such fora can be temporary, ad hoc, or permanent, and vary with the issue and scope of the collective action problem.

Finally, a constitutional pact would create or empower institutions of last resort with the capacity to interpret, apply, and enforce constitutional norms, ideally on a nonconsensual basis. A constitutional court of last resort is important for settling constitutional disagreements, but also for ensuring the consistency and coherence of international law as a whole by serving as a court of appeals. A court of last resort could offer the possibility of appealing a decision taken by the range of courts operating in international law, resolve disagreements among lower courts on the proper interpretation of regular treaties, and ensure that such interpretation is consistent with constitutional essentials. A constitutional court would stand apart from and check the power of the collection of decision-making bodies empowered by a constitution, in order to limit majoritarian abuse and usurpation of minority rights, which is an especially strong danger for decisions taken on such a large scale.

Global constitutionalization is likely to come about, if it does at all, through a process which requires persuasion, negotiation, compromise, and revision. It will require intermediate transition steps to allow states to gradually develop a shared vision of an international rule of law. To get off the ground, a constitutionalized international law will have to rely on a critical mass of states, likely those with a stronger constitutional tradition and other willing states, to lay the groundwork for a new constitutional order for international law. In time, the constitutional pact could expand to ultimately include the entire international community by acquiring moral legitimacy as the best framework for governing international law and by providing practical benefits that individuals and states will have reason to value.

Besides its important rule-of-law features and substantive rules which protect order and human rights at the global level, one appealing consequence of this modest form of constitutionalism is that states will be left to their own devices for most other areas of international law, as they have been so far, and they will continue to be bound by ordinary treaty law only with consent. Thus, global constitutionalism has strong "pluralism preserving" features: outside of the constitution, the diversity of states' goals, interests, values, and cultures can be reflected in their assumptions of differential baskets of legal obligations under international law. Therefore, most international law can still operate under the principle Richard Bellamy calls "differentiated integration," which in the context of the EU has allowed member states to opt out of or give a different interpretation in national law to European-level rules and directives (Bellamy 2019, 174–207).

Still, one of the reasons legal pluralists push back against constitutionalism in international law is that it cannot cope with serious social and cultural diversity. Although he does not target this criticism against a possible constitutionalization of international law, James Tully is skeptical of constitutionalism's "pluralism preserving" features. He claims that constitutionalism generates an "empire of uniformity" (Tully 1995, 58–97). Critics see constitutionalism mainly as a tool for integration, which disrupts and overwhelms diverse political, cultural, and religious expressions at the expense of a homogenizing view of law. Niko Krish repeats and reinforces this criticism at the international level. International constitutionalism would mean the acceptance of the "priority of the common" (Krish 2012, 66). While he is more sanguine about the possibility of constitutionalism at the domestic level, and even European one, Krish believes that the kind of radical political and cultural diversity which characterizes international politics is ill-suited for constitutionalization on pluralist grounds. Indeed, constitutionalism means closing the debate on certain legal questions, while "respect for this diversity may require leaving those questions open" (Krish 2012, 68).

Several responses are available to this kind of pluralism-based constitutional skepticism. First, the contrast between pluralism and constitutionalism is overdrawn, as a pluralist interplay of legal orders can function well and is indeed better protected under a constitutional regime (Sweet 2009). Some of the most successful constitutional orders of our time contain rich cultural and religious diversity. To be sure, that diversity is constrained and shaped by constitutional norms, which means that not just any kind of diversity can flourish. But this is much less of a problem than legal pluralists intimate. In international politics, a pluralist order which makes room for genocidal regimes or allows offensive military action which disrupts the functioning of some states by other states without just cause is neither morally acceptable nor as friendly to pluralism as pluralists themselves think. State legal orders, particularly the legal orders of more vulnerable states, are less well protected in the absence of common norms that bind all, including the most powerful states. If the international legal system gives priority to these common rules, it can do so in the name of protecting the boundaries of pluralist legal orders from outside interference and setting minimal standards of acceptability for their functioning. Constitutionally created uniformity is thus necessary for a healthy, morally acceptable form of pluralism, insofar as it creates the space in which a plurality of state legal orders can develop and flourish without permitting them to engage in massive violations of human rights or committing aggression against other legal orders in the system.

As I have shown above, the endorsement of a quasi-absolute form of pluralism is the result of a pluralism without moral foundations. Only once we understand the proper moral limits of pluralism and appreciate that unconstrained pluralism can make room for some of the worst pathologies of social and political life, such as domination of the weak by the strong, lack of commonly agreed constraints on the use of force, and lack of respect for shared standards of individual rights, can we better appreciate the benefits of a constitutional order. Krish is worried of course that "constitutionalism is in a constant tension with changing social circumstances" (2012, 78). But minimal moral and legal rules which secure peace, restrain violence, and protect rights ought to be valid regardless of changing circumstances. This holds true at the international level as much as at the domestic one. Consequently, the constitutionalism I am defending is no blueprint for an "empire of uniformity." It is a blueprint for minimal decency and mutual toleration.

Generally speaking, if one does not already accept the benefits of domestic constitutional orders, one will be less likely to accept constitutionalism as a structural improvement at the international level, and may insist, with Krish, that the adaptability, openness, and flexibility of pluralism should win the day (2012, 70). But surely this depends to a very large extent on the goodwill, adaptability, and flexibility of the component parts of the pluralist order, and many states today are anything but willing to participate in mechanisms for resolving conflicts that are flexible, adaptable, or open to contestation. As a practical matter, flexibility, adaptability, and contestation among legal orders are easier to achieve when they share a background of legal values and principles and share institutional mechanisms which embed flexibility and contestation, as constitutional orders do. But it becomes problematic to rely on pluralism when there is no good-faith recognition among political officials in the various state-based legal orders of the rights and interests of their citizens, or the rights and interests of other states and of their citizens.

In fact, Krish acknowledges these weaknesses when he says that pluralism "may be highly beneficial in benign circumstances, when the relevant actors show the required disposition for responding to argument and exchanging experiences and knowledge." Thus, "pluralism's greater adaptability may thus be a virtue only in certain, potentially quite limited conditions" (Krish 2012, 81). Unless Krish believes that those empirical conditions which make pluralism desirable are met at the international level, there is little basis for advancing it as a plausible alternative to constitutionalism.

Nonetheless, I would go even further and reject pluralism even in the ideal conditions Krish describes, those of overlapping legal orders willing to engage one another in argument, mutual toleration, and open contestation. As I showed in chapter 3, the international rule of law demands that political power is bound by law, at both the state and international levels; powerful states are held to similar standards as weaker ones; and access to legal justice through courts is guaranteed for all those whose rights and interests are protected by the international legal order, including individuals and nonstate actors. Thomas Christiano (2020) has argued recently that there is something prima facie unjust about the fact that international criminal law is to a large extent optional, and that states avoid accountability for the most serious international crimes by opting out of the jurisdiction of the ICC. If one agrees with this diagnosis, as I do, the justification for making structural changes to make these international rule-of-law ideals a reality becomes more salient, and pluralism offers no support for the changes required to implement them.

Constitutionalism of the modest sort I advocate will leave many global problems unsolved. In that sense Krish is right that unless one goes for a very demanding form of constitutionalism, one that promises to refashion every political structure in the world, including states, along standards of popular sovereignty and liberal democratic values, we will be left with large- and small-scale oppression and human rights violations, autocratic regimes, and problems of domination within and among states (2012, 31–32, 53–57, 104). But it is no argument against constitutionalism at the international level that it does not hold up to the most demanding form of domestic constitutionalism. "Constitutionalism lite'"(Krish 2012, 57–58) would be a huge step forward and not a capitulation to the status quo, even if it reveals a big gap between certain political ideals and the present context. Krish's comparative institutional analysis, while laudable in its aims, does not set up a fair contest; he holds constitutionalism to standards that pluralism cannot meet. Unconstrained legal pluralism represents a much bigger capitulation, since it does not put forward a political ideal of its own, except for defending maximal pluralism and a desire to see differences worked out amicably in a system of mutual toleration. In fact, legal pluralism does worse on all of the criteria I mentioned in the beginning of this chapter: it does not solve the legal indeterminacy resulting from problems of competing jurisdiction, it fails to strengthen the rule of law, to increase protection for individual rights, or to protect the autonomy of states from intrusion by other states and international law.

THE UN CHARTER'S QUASI-CONSTITUTIONAL FEATURES

Reservations about further constitutionalizing international law are not limited to legal pluralists. Nonpluralists, also called legal monists, who assert the supremacy of international law, may argue that international law already has the requisite institutional machinery to assert supremacy over national law, and that machinery consists primarily of the UN

Charter, supported by jus cogens norms and the secondary rules of the VCLT. Indeed, some claim that the UN Charter already fulfills the function of a constitution for international law (Fassbender 1998; Sloan 1989; R. Macdonald 2000), and if this were true, adopting a separate constitutional treaty would be redundant.

Indeed, Bardo Fassbender claims that the UN Charter has had a "constitutional quality" from the beginning, and that quality has only strengthened over its first fifty years (and one assumes beyond), as it has evolved into a global constitution (Fassbender 1998, 529). According to Fassbender, a constitution establishes a set of fundamental norms which structure the exercise of political power, it defines the relationship between legal institutions and legal subjects, it provides a legal framework for a community which is stable over time, and it is binding and supreme law. In his view, the UN Charter possesses all of these features (Fassbender 2009, 139–40). He describes the San Francisco conference which gave birth to the Charter as a "constitutional moment" and argues that the Charter enables basic functions of governance of international law through the UN system, that it exercises legal authority over all states, and that it contains supremacy clauses (Fassbender 1998, 568–84). Although describing the Charter as a constitution may appease anxieties about the authority and legitimacy of international law, we have some reasons to be doubtful that the label is apposite, and that to the extent that it contains constitutional elements, they have been institutionalized in the appropriate way.

In negotiating the UN Charter, states did not announce themselves to create a constitution for international law. The primary stated purpose of the Charter was to grant power to a new international organization, namely the United Nations and its several agencies, and to define its rights and privileges. The UN Charter is not that different from charters granted by states to cities, companies, or universities to enable them to function as distinctive legal persons with obligations and entitlements under the law. Even though the Charter is a "constituent treaty" for the UN, it is not a constitutional treaty. It cannot be considered to be a replacement for the constitution of international law as a whole, since much of international law was created and operates outside of the UN system. A constitution for international law would structure the exercise of power within the entire legal system, articulate the nature and limits of the authority of international law over states, and define the general rights and responsibilities of all of its legal subjects. Moreover, the widespread membership of the UN is not sufficient reason to consider the UN Charter constitutional. Other international treaties have near universal membership, such as the Montreal Protocol on Substances which Deplete the Ozone Layer, without thereby becoming constitutions.

The Charter was conceived during a transformative time for international law in the immediate aftermath of World War II, and Fassbender is right to emphasize the many innovations the Charter brought about. But it is one thing to claim that the negotiations leading to the Charter were transformative, and another to claim that due to their transformative nature the end result was a constitution. International law has had other transformative moments before and since, including large-scale decolonization in the 1960s, the creation of the WTO, and the codification of secondary rules for making, changing, and terminating treaties. None of those transformations resulted in constitutions for international law.[7] It would be self-defeating to interpret the idea of a constitutional moment overly broadly to signify any substantive change in a legal system, because large scale change in ordinary law would become indistinguishable from constitutional change.

This is significant, because states have been conscious in avoiding constitutional commitments such as direct effect of the rules of the Charter on national legislation and judicial review of the decisions of national courts. Although the UN Charter contains important quasi-constitutional features which make it less like a regular treaty and more like a constitution, its main purpose was to define and institute a new organ of international law rather than to provide an answer to the thorny question of the proper relationship of states' authority to international law. I will return to these quasi-constitutional features below, but first I would like to emphasize the ways in which the UN Charter fails to be constitutional in the right way.

Among the constitutional features notably absent from the UN Charter are rules articulating a substantive list of human rights and explaining the ways in which these and other moral commitments limit the exercise of political power, especially by states and international organizations. Human rights and other specific requirements of justice, such as rule-of-law principles which ensure access to courts and equality before law, must act as the fundamental moral and legal commitments of international law. In any constitutional system, these moral commitments function as building blocks and provide a yardstick against which the power granted to political institutions is measured. Apart from a passing nod in the preamble of the Charter "to reaffirm faith in fundamental human rights, in the dignity and worth of the human person, in the equal rights of men and women," and a few other vague references throughout the Charter to a mission to promote and encourage respect for human rights (Articles 1, 8, 12, 55, 62, 68, 76), there is little to point to specific human rights as supra-norms of international law which constrain the exercise of political power domestically as well as internationally. The Charter contains no effort to articulate a specific list of human rights or enable mechanisms to encourage their promotion and respect, despite efforts from some states to include a bill of rights in the text when it was negotiated (Nickel 2007, 8). The absence of human rights from the Charter is a reason to question its constitutional credentials. Insofar as articulating and defending human rights is only one of the goals of international law and may be in potential tension with others, a constitutional treaty would need to show a more explicit commitment to human rights as essential elements of an international order and reflect on some of the trade-offs and costs required to uphold them. For example, upholding human rights may be in potential tension with the Charter's preeminent goal of maintaining international peace, when for example severe human rights violations such as genocide might require humanitarian intervention.[8] The Charter does not address and resolve any of these difficult trade-offs.

Another constitutional feature that is noticeably absent from the UN Charter is a compulsory dispute-settlement mechanism empowered to interpret the rules and avoid the situation of states being judges in their own cases. States are often left to interpret their legal obligations under the UN Charter domestically in their respective executive, legislative, and judicial branches. States come to different and even conflicting interpretations of their obligations, and this fact impugns the authority of the Charter as an authoritative legal document. A constitutional court with compulsory jurisdiction would both review member states' actions to ensure compliance with constitutional rules and invalidate the legal acts of international legal bodies which failed to comply with them. While Fassbender acknowledges this failing, he considers it less critical, since "only a minority of states with undoubtedly constitutional systems of government have established courts" which have the power to review regular legislation and limit executive and legislative power (1998, 575). I disagree. I have argued in previous chapters that the lack of a court with compulsory jurisdiction does damage to the ability of international law to ensure stability, coherence, and determinacy; it allows states to extricate themselves from their international legal obligations with impunity; and it generates a permissive climate in which states can take measures both domestically and abroad in conflict with the most important values and principles of international law. Moreover, the absence of a constitutional court leaves the institutions of international law unconstrained and unaccountable, and this feature is especially troubling with respect to the UN enforcement agent, the Security Council, which suffers from several important pathologies which I will return to below. A constitutional court would not be the only plausible mechanism to constrain and limit political power beyond the state, but it is one which is readily available from domestic constitutional models and should be thus seriously considered as a vehicle for institutionalizing a constitutional treaty.

Constitutions also establish hierarchies of norms by placing certain fundamental rules and institutional mechanisms of at the top of the legal order and giving them a preemptive character and direct effect across all subordinate law. In international law, this would mean that the constitution grants fundamental human rights, along with the norms of sovereign equality, noninterference, and the prohibition on the use of force, the role of constraining the action of all other agents operating in the legal system, including states whose norms have superior legal status in their domestic legal systems, and that an international constitutional court is empowered to ascertain violations and demand compliance, much like the Court of Justice of the European Union does for member states (Isiksel 2016). The Charter establishes a hierarchy of norms but only to a certain degree; it asserts the primacy of Charter rules over contrary international law but not municipal law. The Charter creates a partial supremacy of its rules over conflicting international law in Article 103, which says, "In the event of a conflict between the obligations of the Members of the United Nations under the present Charter and their obligations under any other international agreement, their obligations under the present Charter shall prevail." But it does not insist that Charter rules prevail over conflicting municipal law. Article 2, paragraph 6 requires the organization of the UN through its Security Council to secure the compliance of nonmembers (and one assumes members) "so far as may be necessary for the maintenance of international peace and security." Yet this generates a rather vaguely defined power for the Security Council, which enjoys vast interpretive leeway, and can choose to always ignore serious human rights violations ostensibly in the name of and for the sake of international peace. This problem of partial supremacy leaves unresolved the fundamental tension between the two claims of legal supremacy made by national and international law. As I explained at length in chapter 4, such tension poses an existential threat to international law and undermines its authority and legitimacy.

As is becoming clear, the Charter contains quasi-constitutional features among its rules by codifying several fundamental principles of international law, but even when it does so, the rules are so vague as to leave room for almost absolute discretion from states. Among the most important principles codified in the Charter are arguably sovereign equality, the prohibition on the use of force, and the principle of noninterference (Article 1). The last of these is translated in Article 2, paragraph 4, in the principle which requires states to "refrain in their international relations from the threat or use of force against the territorial integrity or political independence of any state." Yet further in paragraph 7, the Charter states, "Nothing contained in the present Charter shall authorize the United Nations to intervene in matters which are essentially within the domestic jurisdiction of any state or shall require the Members to submit such matters to settlement under the present Charter." Paragraphs 4 and 7 stipulate noninterference as a principle of sovereign autonomy. They give wide berths to states to pursue their domestic sovereign prerogatives without interference from the outside.

Yet notice that the Charter fails to explain what is considered "essentially within the domestic jurisdiction of any state." Without further interpretive work, the principle of noninterference is left vague and almost inoperable. States are tempted to interpret paragraph 7 in the broadest way possible so that any interference with their sovereign prerogative is deemed unjustified. Indeed, states have done so repeatedly in order to resist calls to invoke Security Council Chapter VII powers to intervene on the territory of other states who pose a threat to international peace or engage in large-scale violations of the rights of their citizens. Due to the imprecise nature of the Charter language, the norm of noninterference comes into conflict with other Charter norms and other norms of international law, such as the prohibition against genocide, and this conflict renders international law indeterminate with respect to some of its most basic rules. One could argue that the role of courts is precisely to resolve this kind of indeterminacy, yet the ICJ is not in a position to do so due to the fact that its authority is consent based, and states have been reluctant to cede it power with respect to this and other conflicts of interpretation stemming from Charter rules. Thus, while the Charter defines essential rules for the maintenance of international peace, these rules tend to be indeterminate, and compulsory mechanisms for resolving the indeterminacy by interpreting and applying the rules in contexts where they are pertinent are absent.

The lack of a court with compulsory jurisdiction does not stand alone among the shortcomings of institutionalizing the UN Charter. One could make the case that one of the most serious defects of the Charter is granting vast powers to use force to an agency that is unaccountable and whose membership and decision structure privilege some countries at the expense of others. The Security Council contains five countries which are permanent members with veto power (China, Russia, France, the United Kingdom, and the United States), whereas ten other countries can rotate into two-year positions without veto power for a total of fifteen members. As Michael Doyle emphasizes, "council decisions are binding on all UN members (arts 25 and 48) when they garner the requisite nine votes," but the permanent members have a special status; they "have the unequal right to remain unbound unless they concur or abstain" (2009, 118). Such a structure cements inequality of power with respect to the voice of various members of the UN, and the consequent lack of impartiality renders the Security Council morally illegitimate as the ultimate enforcer of the UN Charter.

Article 24, paragraph 1 justifies the authority of the Security Council in terms of effectiveness:

> In order to ensure prompt and effective action by the United Nations, its Members confer on the Security Council primary responsibility for the maintenance of international peace and security, and agree that in carrying out its duties under this responsibility the Security Council acts on their behalf.

Yet it is far from clear why this particular structure of the Security Council is justified on grounds of effectiveness. The justification based on effectiveness may have had some purchase at the end of a catastrophic international war, when co-opting major powers into an international enforcement mechanism will have made practical sense as a way to give them a forum to negotiate their disagreements and express their differing views on the priorities of the international community. But it is also clear that these differences have often led to deadlocks and an inability to act, and that the permanent members often act in ways that further their own narrow interests at the expense of important goals of the international community and the observance of the primary rules of international law, problems which should seriously undermine any contemporary attempts to ground the structure of the Security Council in reasons of effectiveness.

Consider the obligation for members stated in Article 33, paragraph 1:

> The parties to any dispute, the continuance of which is likely to endanger the maintenance of international peace and security, shall, first of all, seek a solution by negotiation, enquiry, mediation, conciliation, arbitration, judicial settlement, resort to regional agencies or arrangements, or other peaceful means of their own choice.

States regularly violate this obligation, and the Security Council has had an important role to play in pressuring countries to seek peaceful dispute resolution mechanisms. It has demanded that countries involved in international conflicts, such as the Chad and Libya, which were trapped in a long-running military dispute over the Aouzou strip, resolve their disagreements before the ICJ. Chad and Libya did so successfully in 1994. The Security Council has had an important role to play in diffusing tensions involving the use of military force with potentially devastating regional and international consequences in the Corfu Chanel case, which involved a dispute between Albania and the United Kingdom about the status of a strait (ICJ 1949). But when the violators are the permanent members of the Security Council, or when international crimes involve their political and economic interests, they can use their veto power to sanction illegality, to avoid fulfilling their own obligations, or to resist accountability when the fact of violation has been established. The Security Council has refused to enforce the judgment of the ICJ, which found the US in violation of the principle of noninterference in the *Nicaragua v. US* (1986) case, while it has enforced the decisions of the ICJ in other cases of noncompliance (Morrison 1987). Russia and China have repeatedly blocked attempts in the Security Council to create a no-fly zone in Syria during the worst part of the civil war and any other resolutions aimed at protecting civilians, largely due to their economic and political interests in the area (Macfarquhar and Shadid 2012; Morris 2012). And China refuses to acknowledge the jurisdiction of the arbitration court, which found it in violation of the law of the sea in the South China Sea, no doubt in part encouraged by the fact that it can block any Security Council resolution requesting that it comply with it (Phillips, Holmes, and Bowcott 2016). All of these examples show that the permanent members use their status within the Security Council to overlook serious violations of international law when they stand to benefit and to avoid accountability for their own violations. The inequality embedded in the formal structure of the Security Council divides the world into those to whom international law applies and those to whom it does not, thus undermining an essential principle in any legal system, that of equality under the law. Consequently, the Security Council cannot function as an acceptable constitutional mechanism of enforcement for international law.[9]

The most damning evidence *against* the claim that the international system is constitutionalized comes from states' continuous assertion of legal supremacy of domestic constitutional rules over contrary international law. As long as states themselves refuse to see the international system as a constitutional legal order to which they must give priority for rules crucial to international peace and justice, there is little chance that it can be described and interpreted as such, the pronouncements of prominent international legal scholars to the contrary notwithstanding. The functionalist approach preferred by Fassbender allows a constitutional order to evolve so elusively and mysteriously that legal subjects are gradually made part of a constitutional order without their consent or awareness. Yet how can we have an international constitutional order if no domestic legal order understands itself to be bound by it? A constitutional order cannot sneak up on its subjects but must be to an important extent deliberately created and affirmed by them.

In the end, I agree with Doyle's verdict that the UN Charter is more than a regular treaty but less than a constitution (Doyle 2009). Still, the point I have been pressing so far is stronger: while the UN Charter does exhibit some constitutional features, these features are poorly designed and institutionalized. Rather than claim that international law is already constitutionalized, it would be more accurate to claim that it is in the process of constitutionalization, with some important quasi-constitutional elements imbedded in the Charter, jus cogens, and VCLT, but others clearly missing or incomplete. This leaves two options: either the Charter is substantially revised and converted into a proper constitutional treaty, or a new stand-alone constitutional treaty is created. The second option is preferable, as it would be helpful to further disentangle the role of the Charter as a grant of authority to the United Nations from its role as an international constitution. I have only outlined the most essential elements of an adequate constitutional design at the international level and left open what possible options remain on the table within the constraints thus outlined. Outlining the constitutional design options will constitute a research project on its own. But the structural health, authority, and legitimacy of international law will depend on its being carried out successfully.

CONCLUSION

Constitutional language is fashionable in international law scholarship, although currently it serves to mask rather than expose important structural problems such as legal indeterminacy, conflicting rules, and lack of accountability for powerful states. It also serves a positive role: it is a rhetorical strategy designed to buttress international law's legitimacy in the face of anxieties created by worries about eroding domestic democratic control or backlash against the human rights standards which place constraints on authoritarian rule. But this positive role cannot be fulfilled unless the rhetoric more closely matches the reality of international law. This involves delivering on its constitutional promise: that of creating a system that generates a legal hierarchy which places individual and state rights at its core and empowers and limits institutions tasked with protecting them. In the process of negotiating a new constitutional compromise with these features, sovereign states will better define the nature and scope of authority of international law over them and will demonstrate more convincingly their commitment to a system of international law based on justice.

REFERENCES

Altman, Andrew, and Christopher Heath Wellman. 2004. "A Defense of International Criminal Law." *Ethics* 115 (1): 35–67.

Barnett, Michael. 2003. *Eyewitness to a Genocide: The United Nations and Rwanda.* Ithaca, NY: Cornell University Press.

Bellamy, Richard. 2019. *A Republican Europe of States: Cosmopolitanism, Intergovernmentalism and Democracy in the EU.* Cambridge, UK: Cambridge University Press.

Berman, Paul. 2007. "A Pluralist Approach to International Law." *Yale Journal of International Law* 32 (2). http://digitalcommons.law.yale.edu/yjil/vol32/iss2/3.

Berman, Paul Schiff. 2006. "Global Legal Pluralism." *Southern California Law Review* 80: 1155.

Chang, Ruth. 1998. *Incommensurability, Incomparability, and Practical Reason.* Cambridge, MA: Harvard University Press.

Christiano, Thomas. 2020. "The Arbitrary Circumscription of the Jurisdiction of the International Criminal Court." *Critical Review of International Social and Political Philosophy* 23 (3): 352–70.

Cohen, Jean L. 2012. *Globalization and Sovereignty: Rethinking Legality, Legitimacy, and Constitutionalism.* Cambridge, UK: Cambridge University Press.

Cover, Robert M. 1983. "Foreword: Nomos and Narrative." *Harvard Law Review* 97: 4.

Cover, Robert M. 1984. "The Folktales of Justice: Tales of Jurisdiction." *Capital University Law Review* 14: 179.

Criddle, Evan J., and Evan Fox-Decent. 2009. "A Fiduciary Theory of Jus Cogens." *Yale Journal of International Law* 34: 331–87.

Crowder, George. 2004. *Isaiah Berlin: Liberty, Pluralism and Liberalism.* Cambridge, UK: Polity Press.

Deitelhoff, Nicole. 2009. "The Discursive Process of Legalization: Charting Islands of Persuasion in the ICC Case." *International Organization* 63 (01): 33–65.

Djeffal, Christian. 2013. "Commentaries on the Law of Treaties: A Review Essay Reflecting on the Genre of Commentaries." *European Journal of International Law* 24 (4): 1223–38.

Dovi, Suzanne. 2002. "Preferable Descriptive Representatives: Will Just Any Woman, Black, or Latino Do?" *American Political Science Review* 96 (4): 729–43.

Doyle, Michael W. 2009. "The UN Charter—A Global Constitution?" In *Ruling the World? Constitutionalism, International Law, and Global Governance*, edited by Jeffrey L. Dunoff and Joel P. Trachtman, 113–32. Cambridge, UK: Cambridge University Press.

Dunoff, Jeffrey L. 2009. "The Politics of International Constitutions: The Curious Case of the World Trade Organization." In *Ruling the World? Constitutionalism, International Law, and Global Governance*, edited by Jeffrey L. Dunoff and Joel P. Trachtman, 178–205. Cambridge, UK: Cambridge University Press.

Dunoff, Jeffrey L., and Joel P. Trachtman, eds. 2009a. *Ruling the World? Constitutionalism, International Law, and Global Governance*. Cambridge, UK: Cambridge University Press.

Dunoff, Jeffrey L., and Joel P. Trachtman. 2009b. "A Functional Approach to International Constitutionalization." In *Ruling the World? Constitutionalism, International Law, and Global Governance*, edited by Jeffrey L. Dunoff and Joel P. Trachtman, 3–35. Cambridge, UK: Cambridge University Press.

Fassbender, Bardo. 1998. "The United Nations Charter As Constitution of the International Community." *Columbia Journal of Transnational Law* 36: 529.

Fassbender, Bardo. 2009. "Rediscovering the Forgotten Constitution: Notes on the Place of the UN Charter in the International Legal Order." In *Ruling the World? Constitutionalism, International Law, and Global Governance*, edited by Jeffrey L. Dunoff and Joel P. Trachtman, 133–47. Cambridge, UK: Cambridge University Press.

Fitzmaurice, Gerald. 1957. *The General Principles of International Law Considered from the Standpoint of the Rule of Law*, Collected Courses of the Hague Academy of International law, (Volume 92). Hague: Brill | Nijhoff.

Hart, H. L. A. 2012. *The Concept of Law*. 3rd ed. Edited by Leslie Green. Oxford: Oxford University Press.

Hurd, Ian. 2015. "The International Rule of Law and the Domestic Analogy." *Global Constitutionalism* 4 (3): 365–95.

Isiksel, Turkuler. 2016. *Europe's Functional Constitution: A Theory of Constitutionalism Beyond the State*. Oxford: Oxford University Press.

Kadelbach, Stefan. 2006. "Jus Cogens, Obligations Erga Omnes and Other Rules—the Identification of Fundamental Norms." In *The Fundamental Rules of the International Legal Order:* Jus Cogens *and Obligations* Erga Omnes, edited by Christian Tomuschat and Jean-Marc Thouvenin, 21–41. Hague: Brill Nijhoff.

Kekes, John. 1996. *The Morality of Pluralism*. Princeton, NJ: Princeton University Press.

Klabbers, Jan, Anne Peters, and Geir Ulfstein. 2009. *The Constitutionalization of International Law*. Oxford: Oxford University Press.

Koskenniemi, Martti. 2007. "The Fate of Public International Law: Between Technique and Politics." *Modern Law Review* 70 (1): 1–30.

Krish, Nico. 2012. *Beyond Constitutionalism: The Pluralist Structure of Postnational Law*. Oxford: Oxford University Press.

Kumm, Mattias. 2005. "The Jurisprudence of Constitutional Conflict: Constitutional Supremacy in Europe before and after the Constitutional Treaty." *European Law Journal* 11 (3): 262–307.

Kuper, Andrew. 2004. *Democracy Beyond Borders: Justice and Representation in Global Institutions*. New York: Oxford University Press.

Larmore, Charles E. 1987. *Patterns of Moral Complexity*. New York: Cambridge University Press.

Lefkowitz, David. 2017. "What Makes a Social Order Primitive? In Defense of Hart's Take on International Law." *Legal Theory* 23 (4): 258–82.

Lipson, Charles. 1991. "Why Are Some International Agreements Informal?" *International Organization* 45 (4): 495–538.

Macdonald, Ronald. 2000. "The Charter of the United Nations as a World Constitution." *International Law Studies* 75 (1): 263–300.

Macdonald, Terry. 2008. *Global Stakeholder Democracy: Power and Representation Beyond Liberal States*. New York: Oxford University Press.

Macfarquhar, Neil, and Anthony Shadid. 2012. "Russia and China Block U.N. Action on Syrian Crisis." *New York Times*, February 4.

Mansbridge, Jane. 2003. "Rethinking Representation." *American Political Science Review* 97 (04): 515–28.

Morris, Harvey. 2012. "Russia's Reasons for Saying 'No' on Syria." *International Herald Tribune*. January 31.

Morrison, Fred L. 1987. "Legal Issues in the Nicaragua Opinion." *American Journal of International Law* 81 (1): 160–66.

Nickel, James. 2007. *Making Sense of Human Rights*. 2nd ed. Oxford: Wiley-Blackwell.

Nollkaemper, André. 2013. "Inside or Out : Two Types of International Legal Pluralism." In *Normative Pluralism and International Law: Exploring Global Governance*, edited by Jan Klabbers and Touko Piiparinen, 94–140. Cambridge: Cambridge University Press.

Pavel, Carmen. 2015. *Divided Sovereignty: International Institutions and the Limits of State Authority*. Oxford: Oxford University Press.

Pavel, Carmen E. 2018. "Is International Law a Hartian Legal System?" *Ratio Juris* 31 (3): 307–25.

Pellet, Alain. 2013. "The ILC Guide to Practice on Reservations to Treaties: A General Presentation by the Special Rapporteur." *European Journal of International Law* 24 (4): 1061–97.

Phillips, Tom, Oliver Holmes, and Owen Bowcott. 2016. "Beijing Rejects Tribunal's Ruling in South China Sea Case." *Guardian*, July 12, sec. World news. https://www.theguardian.com/world/2016/jul/12/philippines-wins-south-china-sea-case-against-china.

Ratner, Steven. 2013. "Ethics and International Law: Integrating the Global Justice Project(s)." *International Theory* 5 (1): 1–34.

Ratner, Steven. 2019. "International Law and Political Philosophy: Uncovering New Linkages." *Philosophy Compass* 14 (2): e12564.

Ratner, Steven R. 2015. *The Thin Justice of International Law: A Moral Reckoning of the Law of Nations*. Oxford: Oxford University Press.

Ratner, Steven R., and Anne-Marie Slaughter. 2004. *The Methods of International Law*. Washington, DC American Society of International Law.

Rehfeld, Andrew. 2005. *The Concept of Constituency: Political Representation, Democratic Legitimacy, and Institutional Design*. New York: Cambridge University Press.

Sloan, Blaine. 1989. "The United Nations Charter as a Constitution." *Pace International Law Review* 1 (1): 61.

Stewart, James G., and Asad Kiyani. 2017. "The Ahistoricism of Legal Pluralism in International Criminal Law." *American Journal of Comparative Law* 65 (2): 393–449.

Stone, Peter. 2011. *The Luck of the Draw: The Role of Lotteries in Decision Making*. Oxford: Oxford University Press.

Suami, Takao, Anne Peters, Dimitri Vanoverbeke, and Mattias Kumm, eds. 2018. *Global Constitutionalism from European and East Asian Perspectives*. Cambridge, UK: Cambridge University Press.

Sweet, Alec Stone. 2009. "Constitutionalism, Legal Pluralism, and International Regimes." *Indiana Journal of Global Legal Studies* 16 (2). https://works.bepress.com/alec_stone_sweet/27/.

Thouvenin, Christian Tomuschat; Jean-Marc, eds. 2005. *The Fundamental Rules of the International Legal Order:* Jus Cogens *and Obligations* Erga Omnes. Hague: Brill Nijhoff.

Tully, James. 1995. *Strange Multiplicity: Constitutionalism in an Age of Diversity.* Cambridge, UK: Cambridge University Press.

Weiler, J. H. H. 2003. "In Defense of the Status Quo, Europe's Constitutional Sonderweg." In *European Constitutionalism beyond the State*, edited by J. H. H. Weiler and Marlene Wind, 7–24. Cambridge, UK: Cambridge University Press.

Conclusion

International law operates at some remove from our everyday lives, and because we do not ordinarily confront it as we confront domestic and local rules, we are tempted to misjudge how deeply it matters to our lives and to the robustness of our political communities. Rules regulating the use of force, those protecting bedrock human rights, dividing up territory and resources and facilitating coordination, cooperation, and the resolution of collective action problems across borders are crucial components of a peaceful and just international order and of a peaceful and just domestic order. This book makes the case that we must appreciate the profound ways in which international law transforms the relationship states have to their citizens and to one another.

Two major overlapping trends have marked the evolution of international law in the last 80 years: legalization and institutionalization. Legalization has consisted in the creation of vast numbers of international treaties for managing resources in the global commons, such as the prevention of ocean pollution by oil tankers and the preservation of straddling fish stocks, those enabling international transport and telecommunication, the trade in goods and services, and the protection of vulnerable individuals from their governments. In parallel to legalization, new institutions have been created to manage, apply, and enforce treaty rules, from the UN system, to the WTO, the Law of the Sea regime, regional human rights courts such as the Interamerican Court of Human Rights and the European Court of Human Rights, and the International Criminal

Law Beyond the State. Carmen E. Pavel, Oxford University Press (2021). © Oxford University Press.
DOI: 10.1093/oso/9780197543894.003.0007

Court. The institutions created are often weak in the face of state ambivalence or indifference but have made important progress in articulating and stabilizing states' legal obligations, resolving disputes, and laying the groundwork for a more lasting international peace.

That states create institutions, then fail to comply with their rules, withdraw from them, or simply choose to ignore their authority, shows how hesitant the former are to committing to reciprocal constraints on their sovereignty. The relationship states have to international law is best understood as a paradox of commitment. States and their citizens would benefit if other states would observe certain rules and restrictions in their behavior toward each other, but each state would prefer that it retain maximal freedom to act unconstrained by such rules. Revealing that paradox has been one of the main aims of this book. The final chapters sketch a proposal for how to resolve this problem of commitment. A constitutional agreement consisting of the basic principles and rules of interaction among states can offer a way out of this paradox. A constitutional agreement holds the potential, or so I argue, to iron out conflicts between domestic and international legal orders; to introduce more robust rule-of-law protections for various agents operating in international politics; to create more reliable, nonoptional mechanisms for legal accountability; to protect a moral minimum of rights for individuals and states; and to generate authoritative mechanisms for the resolution of collective action problems.

This proposal is in some ways overly ambitious and in other ways not as ambitious as it might seem at first glance. It is overly ambitious because we are undergoing a period of retrenchment from international cooperation and an attitude of anti-internationalism accompanied by the weakening of liberal democratic institutions domestically. This might not seem like the time to place faith in the ability of states to identify and act on their common interests and the interests of their citizens. During the best of times for international institutions, states seem unwilling to commit to long-lasting restrictions on their sovereignty.

But there is already a solid basis in international law to move closer to a constitutional pact. At least since the creation of the UN Charter, international law has evolved a series of quasi-constitutional features on which a constitutional agreement can build. Among them are the principles of sovereign equality, noninterference, and restrictions on the use of force; absolute prohibitions against a series of crimes considered to be of interest to the international community as a whole (jus cogens norms); and the nonoptional legal authority of the Security Council's decisions. The Charter itself is the source of some of these principles, along with the Geneva Conventions, various human rights treaties, the VCLT, and customary law. A new constitutional agreement would develop and specify those principles to ensure greater consistency across the various basic rules of international law (for example by resolving the tension between the principle of noninterference on the one hand, and prohibitions against large-scale rights violations which occasionally give rise to military intervention on the other); would create more robust mechanisms for their interpretation, application, and enforcement; and would facilitate agreement on procedures for resolving collective action problems such as climate change. More importantly, it could better manage, and perhaps dissolve to some extent, the conflict between two claims of legal supremacy, those of domestic legal orders and international law, which is a defining feature of the relationship states have to international law today.

Discussed in chapter 4, this conflict between two claims of legal supremacy ultimately undermines the power of international rules which are essential for a peaceful global order. Domestic constitutional orders assign institutions with final authority over the territory of a state, and these institutions can reject the authority of the rules and institutions of international law which apply to the same territory. The most important expression of this conflict in international law is found in the overreliance on state consent as a basis for the authority of international legal rules and institutions. The reliance on a contractual paradigm for law making and law enforcement results in many of the basic rules of international law being optional, due to states' withholding consent either for the rules themselves or for the institutions which interpret and apply them. Consent preserves state legal autonomy, just as contract law in domestic legal systems preserves the legal autonomy of individual subjects, but it must be exercised against a background of nonoptional rules which give consent its moral and legal force, namely rules which protect the autonomy of the contracting parties, prevent coercion and undue pressure, and ensure that disputes arising from the nonperformance of contracts can be settled peacefully and equitably.

The overreliance on state consent, coupled with other features of international law, gives rise to serious structural failings in its current operation. Among them are the fact that international law lacks rule-of-law protections for smaller, less powerful states. Nonstate actors suffer the effects of harmful state action but lack access to accountability mechanisms. Therefore, the proposal of a constitutional pact among states might not seem ambitious enough. It will leave many imbalances of power among states unaddressed, and small and large injustices individuals and nonstate actors suffer routinely will not find a resolution. Yet it is important to not make the best the enemy of the good. A constitutional agreement will not fix all problems; however, it will address some major structural shortcomings of international law.

While the book draws on international legal scholarship, legal philosophy, and empirical and qualitative political science, its mode of analysis distinguishes it as a work of political philosophy. It evaluates and diagnoses the relationship states have to international law and proposes guidelines for institutional reform at the international level. It identifies some of the central moral ideals of the rule of law and places them at the core of a revised international legal system. It seeks to ensure that the subjects of international law stand in a relationship of equality and autonomy, and that the institutions which make, interpret, and apply rules are confined to their legitimate sphere of authority. The ultimate beneficiaries of a revised international law are the individuals living in various states. Their interests are better protected when states respect human rights, cooperate peacefully, refrain from producing negative externalities which cross borders, and protect natural resources. The political philosophy that I am drawn to is one which takes individuals as the ultimate units of moral concern, and this book demonstrates that normative analyses of international law can be substantially enriched by taking this perspective.

In its reformist mood, political philosophy can be unsettling. It disrupts the status quo by highlighting flaws in the organization of political life and by advancing proposals for change, proposals which themselves carry risks of failure. As Sharon Krause, one of my intellectual mentors, once said, political philosophy is like fixing a ship while at sea. You must do the necessary repairs while meeting the challenge of staying afloat and making the journey to your final destination as comfortable as possible. Constitutionalizing international law is an ambitious project of navigating more adroitly the treacherous waters of international politics. And it carries with it the risks of poor design, co-optation by special interests, increased domination, and corruption. However, no project of institutional reform is free of those risks, and they must always be balanced against the possible benefits of making international law more just, more robust, and less likely to favor powerful states.

Legal systems are successful not only to the extent that they engender peaceful cooperation, but also to the extent that they protect the vulnerable against the powerful. Endowing international law with rule-of-law-like features through constitutionalization could potentially reduce, without eliminating, the exposure of less powerful, developing states to the interferences and undue pressures of larger, more developed ones, by codifying equality before the law, ensure that institutions which interpret and apply the law are more responsive to the former groups' interests and concerns, and hold all states accountable for the violation of the most basic rules of international cooperation.

Cynics and skeptics will resist these conclusions. They will disagree with the diagnosis of the failings of international law or with the proposal for reform. They will point to the decline in pro-internationalist attitudes among political leaders and publics swayed by populist and nationalist rhetoric. They will emphasize the self-interested attitude of powerful states and the reluctance of less powerful states to engage in a process of negotiation and compromise in which they do not have guarantees that their interests and voices will be taken seriously. All of these reasons for skepticism point to an unwillingness to challenge or change the status quo and an unavoidable conservatism about institutional reform.

My aim is not to dismiss these concerns. They are rooted in real difficulties, biases, and features of our world that we ought to consider carefully. Awareness of these features should shape both institutional design and strategies for getting skeptics and cynics on board, but it must not lead us to abandon the goal of creating a more just, legitimate, and robust system of international law. Accepting the status quo would require making peace with large inequalities in the relations among states, with vast human rights violations committed within states, with uncertainty in international politics, and with inconsistency in international law.

This is why further institutionalization of international law is needed. A constitutional pact is not a superfluous superposition on a perfectly functional international legal system, but a way to make the system more coherent, more just, and more effective. We need a constitution and courts with compulsory jurisdiction at the international level for the same reason we need them at the domestic level: to articulate the principles and value commitments of the international community, to create orders of priority among legal rules, and to authorize dispute-resolution mechanisms which interpret the rules and solve disagreements among states. While quasi-constitutional rules are already present in international law, their status is contested, they sometimes come into conflict with one another, and states are frequently left to their own devices to interpret and apply them.

Legalization and institutionalization are not ends in themselves. More law is not better, and its proliferation can create insidious bureaucracies and superfluous power structures. But when the rules continue to be ambiguous and states are often left to interpret their international obligations by themselves, this worry seems unfounded for the current state of international law. Strengthening institutions which solidify rule-of-law protections for small and big states alike, as well as for individuals and other agents likely to be directly affected by the rules of international law, is imperative.

One could read my argument to render international law more robust in one of two ways: either (1) make existing rules and institutions more authoritative and efficacious, or (2) create new international rules to better safeguard peace, defend human rights, combat climate change, and foster cooperation. My focus is on 1, but I do not think that getting states to better comply with their existing legal obligations can be accomplished without 2. States have already created a vast range of treaties and customary rules to negotiate territorial space, respect human rights, extradite suspected criminals, coordinate telecommunication and mailing services, and govern global commons. And they have created courts and institutions whose role is to institute those rules. The rules and institutions cover vast areas of international cooperation and address issues which states regularly confront in their interactions with each other and their citizens or the citizens of other countries. Making these more robust, such that states would comply more readily with existing international law, would go a long way toward addressing outstanding, critical problems in international politics, such as large-scale abuses of human rights.

However, international law suffers from serious gaps as well, in areas such as refugee protection, the protection of indigenous groups and minority rights, and the management of global resources and global commons. Climate change is just one of the issues for which solutions have been intractable, and other collective action problems are still insufficiently addressed. To make solutions to these collective action problems possible, as well as improve the observance of existing international legal rules, I propose challenging some of the structural features of international law, such as the overreliance on state consent, the absence of courts with compulsory jurisdiction, and resolving jurisdictional conflicts between domestic and international law via a new constitutional compact. This would go some way toward making existing rules more robust, since the new constitutional compact would rely in large measure on existing rules of international law which have a quasi-constitutional feature.

International law transforms state authority by both limiting and empowering sovereign autonomy. It limits autonomy by requiring states to observe restrictions on the permissible ways they can interact with their citizens and other states. And it empowers autonomy to the extent that states can more effectively pursue their goals without interference from other states. While states have the means of creating a stronger system of rights protection for both states and individuals and for solving a variety of cooperation problems, they lack the will to do so. Constitutionalization is a means of creating the will. It enables states to commit anew to secondary international legal rules—rules about how to make rules—and to settle disagreement about such rules.

The quasi-constitutional norms that exist today, such as the norms of sovereignty, equality, and noninterference; jus cogens norms; and prohibitions on the use of force, are substantive, not institutional norms. One might be skeptical that institutionalizing them, that is, creating institutions whose roles is to further specify, apply, and enforce them, is necessary and that it will not interfere with the authority of sovereign states to protect their interests and set their own goals. Nonetheless, existing substantive norms are not self-enforcing, and states disagree on their meaning routinely. For example, states disagree whether the norm of noninterference protects states even when they commit horrendous abuses against their own citizens—that is, on whether humanitarian intervention is justified—or whether the self-defense exception from the prohibition on the use of force can be interpreted to allow preventive war. It is these interpretive and other disagreements which render international law powerless in the face of states stretching the meaning of legal rules, often hypocritically. Since the substance of these basic rules of international law is not settled by impartial, authoritative institutions, the margin of interpretation remains wide, and states abuse the rules to further their narrow interests at the expense of other states and the international community as a whole.

Further institutionalization is required for international law for the same reason it is required in any complex legal system. Imagine a federal system in which member states would be bound by substantive constitutional rules, but there would be no institutions available to settle diverging and even conflicting interpretation of these rules. Imagine also that member states face conflicts over borders, disagree about basic protections for their citizens, refuse to cooperate to divide water from rivers which cross borders equitably, and engage in racist and other heavily discriminatory practices. Few would argue that agreement on substantive shared norms would be sufficient. The federal arrangement is at risk of unraveling due to major disagreements about how best to interpret and apply the rules among a sufficient number of member states, and military conflict could take the place of peaceful processes of conflict resolution and norm enforcement.

So too in international law, agreement on fundamental norms is not sufficient unless backed by vigorous mechanisms of rule-making, rule interpretation, and enforcement. The point of a vigorous enforcement mechanism is not to heighten division and tensions, but to nudge states into further compliance such that, in time, stronger norms of compliance with international law emerge. Enforcement mechanisms could at a minimum change states' cost-benefit calculations by making noncompliance more costly in a variety of ways (fines, permission for other states to retaliate, temporary cessation of benefits from cooperation, trade boycotts, targeted economic sanctions, etc.).

International law makes legitimate demands on us, both as members of various states, with obligations to minimize the negative effects of our actions across borders, and as potential beneficiaries of its protection. This book has made the case that an appropriately structured and institutionalized international law can do what law does wherever it works well: it emancipates and liberates, protects equality and human dignity, gives expression to individual and common projects, minimizes wrongs, and secures justice. The book constitutes, at the very least, an invitation to contemplate the consequences of taking the project of building international law seriously and to deliberate on the necessary domestic and international institutional changes to make it possible.

NOTES

INTRODUCTION

1. Important exceptions are customary international law and the rules of the UN Charter.
2. For a list of reservations see United Nations Convention on the Prevention and Punishment of the Crime of Genocide (1948) https://treaties.un.org/Pages/ViewDetails.aspx?src=IND&mtdsg_no=IV-1&chapter=4&clang=_en (accessed March 20, 2019).
3. I thank Dan Russell for this important point.

CHAPTER 1

1. All citations to the *Treatise* henceforth are to paragraph numbers.
2. It is important to note that international law does not recognize the validity of all reservations, and the VCLT disqualifies specifically reservations which are incompatible with the "object and purpose of a treaty." See Articles 19–23. But the validity of many reservations remains unsettled since they cannot be disputed without the reserving state's consent.
3. There are significant exceptions to this point; for example, there is scholarly consensus that the rulings of the Court of Justice of the European Union are not optional for member states. See, for example, Kumm (2005) and Isiksel (2016).
4. Several treaties prescribe, either directly or via an additional protocol, courts with compulsory jurisdiction for the rules of that treaty, but only for member states; thus there is no international court with truly compulsory jurisdiction, that is, whose jurisdiction applies to a state without its consent.
5. Jus cogens norms are international norms, such as the prohibition against genocide, crimes against humanity, and slavery, from which derogation is not allowed. Obligations erga omnes are duties states incur as part of the community of states and not simply as individual states agreeing to specific treaties. The four Geneva Conventions are thought to create obligations erga omnes.
6. The Vienna Convention on the Law of Treaties, https://treaties.un.org/doc/Publication/UNTS/Volume%201155/volume-1155-I-18232-English.pdf (accessed April 22, 2017). The important exception to this rule is customary law (Article 38).

7. Monism is typically understood as the position that international and national law are one legal system. Of course, customary law applies without consent (Koh 1997; Maniruzzaman 2001).
8. This why Hume says "Antiquity always begets the opinion of right" in *Of the First Principles of Government* I.IV.3.
9. According to Istvan Hont, Hume was more likely to accept this point by the 1750s–1760s, as his essays "On the Balance of Trade," "On the Balance of Power," and "On the Jealousy of Trade" attest (Hont 2010; Hume 1987).
10. For a more sophisticated account of Hobbes's view of the relationships of law to sovereignty, see Dyzenhaus (2014) and Malcolm (2004, 432–56).
11. Among other things, the Chicago Convention protects state sovereignty over airspace, provides for the multilateral exchange of rights of overflight; regulates customs and emigration; and establishes the International Civil Aviation Organization (ICAO), a UN permanent agency tasked with codifying the principles of international air transport. http://www.icao.int/Meetings/atconf6/Documents/Doc%209626_en.pdf.
12. Sharon Krause has provided several sympathetic reconstructions which avoid the narrowness often associated with Hume's view (Krause 2004, 2010).

CHAPTER 2

1. With important exceptions such as the United States.
2. Marxists and critical theorists seek not only to understand international relations but to also radically transform them. See, for example, R. Gilpin (1987) and Linklater (1990).
3. It is important to note that Mearsheimer and Walt came out against "simplistic" hypothesis testing and in favor of more careful theory building in more recent work (Mearsheimer and Walt 2013).
4. In fact, in the dry Tucson desert, one might prefer to go out in the rain without an umbrella to enjoy the relatively rare experience of falling rain.
5. For a similar account see Grieco (1988, 488).
6. The same is true of an individual who is bent on destruction and killing. Whether the individual is really good at figuring out the best means to kill and plunder says nothing about whether he ought to do it and whether the society should encourage or condone it. The ends of an individual may be immoral (killing for fun), wasteful (gambling), or self-destructive (heavy drinking).
7. This is not a criticism of instrumental rationality as such. Sometimes, one can mistake theoretical conclusions some draw based on instrumental rationality with flaws in the idea of instrumental rationality itself. See (Blau 2011).
8. Parfit even argues that acting consistently self-interested is self-defeating.
9. Rawls used the term *connection* with his two principles of justice.

CHAPTER 3

1. I thank Terry Nardin for this point.
2. For example, the party appoints key members of courts or is able to veto appointments (Peerenboom 2002, 8).

3. The Rule of Law Index, https://worldjusticeproject.org/our-work/wjp-rule-law-index/wjp-rule-law-index-2016 (accessed September 24, 2017), is a project of the nonprofit World Justice Project, set up by the American Bar Association with support from the International Bar Association and other groups.
4. Koskenniemi goes further and claims that the illusion of the rule of law is harmful to the extent to which it encourages "the supremacy of experts and bureaucrats to the detriment of genuine political decisions-making." From E. Jouanet's introduction to *The Politics of International Law* (Koskenniemi 2011, 13, 70–71).
5. Even under treaty law, signatory states do not have the same obligations as other members of the same treaty. The practice of reservations allows states to opt out of certain provisions of a treaty. In customary international law, persistent objectors are states who explicitly and repeatedly claim an exemption from a generally accepted customary rule.
6. Consider also the United States during its westward expansion. New territories, although formally under the jurisdiction of federal law, had weak law, applied unevenly, with courts which were few and far between and under-resourced, and there was little if any supervision of legal officials. See Kenyon (1968, 682–83). International law today shares many of these characteristics.
7. Anthony Anghie, presentation at The Global Rule of Law Conference, Singapore, February 2017.

CHAPTER 4

1. The UN Charter, http://www.un.org/en/charter-united-nations/ (accessed January 1, 2018).
2. See also the debate taking place in Japan upon its accession to the ICC (Meierhenrich and Ko 2009).
3. For CEDAW reservations seehttps://treaties.un.org/Pages/ViewDetails.aspx?src=IND&mtdsg_no=IV-8&chapter=4&lang=en (accessed December 17, 2018). See also Kenneth Roth's critique of the practice of reservations by the United States to human rights treaties, which in his view renders them virtually inapplicable to US citizens (Roth 2000).
4. Even when incorporated into domestic law, international treaties have the same status as federal statutes and are thus lower in the hierarchy compared to constitutional provisions, which means that the constitution remains supreme and trumps any international treaty in case of conflict.
5. The Australian Constitution of 1901, https://www.aph.gov.au/About_Parliament/Senate/Powers_practice_n_procedures/Constitution.aspx (accessed January 1, 2018).
6. Victoria v. Commonwealth—[1996] HCA 56. Paragraph 23: says: "Thus, as matters stand in Australia, and as they stood in 1900, the conduct of external affairs by the Executive may produce agreements which the Executive wishes to translate into the domestic or municipal legal order. To do so, it must procure the passage of legislation implementing those agreements if it wishes to create individual rights and obligations or change existing rights and obligations under that legal order." http://www.austlii.edu.au/cgi-bin/sinodisp/au/cases/cth/HCA/1996/56.html?stem=0&sy

nonyms=0&query=title(victoria%20and%20commonwealth%20) (accessed June 6, 2018).

7. Australia, The Parliament of the Commonwealth of Australia, *Trick or Treaty? Commonwealth Power to Make and Implement Treaties* (report of the Senate Legal and Constitutional References Committee, November 1995), http://www.aph.gov.au/senate/committee/legcon_ctte/treaty/index.htm. See also Australia, Department of Foreign Affairs and Trade, "Government Announces Reform of Treaty-Making," press release, May 2, 1996, http://www.dfat.gov.au/media/releases/foreign/1996/fa29.html; and Commonwealth of Australia, *Review of the Treaty-Making Process* (Canberra, August 1999), http://www.austlii.edu.au/au/other/dfat/reports/review_treaty_making.html. This is a review of the treaty adoption procedure which was developed by the Government of the Commonwealth of Australia and has been in place since 1996.
8. Canada does see itself under an obligation to interpret its constitutional principles and domestic law in such a way as to ensure compliance with its international legal obligations, which lessens the conflict between domestic and international law.
9. The French Constitution of 1958, http://www.conseil-constitutionnel.fr/conseil-constitutionnel/english/constitution/constitution-of-4-october-1958.25742.html (accessed January 1, 2018).
10. The Constitution of the Kingdom of Netherlands of 2008, https://www.government.nl/documents/regulations/2012/10/18/the-constitution-of-the-kingdom-of-the-netherlands-2008 (accessed January 1, 2018).
11. The Basic Law of the Federal Republic of Germany of 1949, https://www.btg-bestellservice.de/pdf/80201000.pdf (accessed January 1, 2018). See also articles 59 and 79.
12. The Spanish Constitution of 1978, http://www.congreso.es/portal/page/portal/Congreso/Congreso/Hist_Normas/Norm/const_espa_texto_ingles_0.pdf (accessed January 1, 2018).
13. The Vienna Convention on the Law of Treaties 1980, https://treaties.un.org/doc/publication/unts/volume%201155/volume-1155-i-18232-english.pdf (accessed January 1, 2018).

CHAPTER 5

1. For example, there is no agreed list of jus cogens norms.
2. Krish helpfully distinguished between constitutions understood as "the sum of the rules and institutions of a society's political system" and constitutions which require separation of powers, judicial review, the protection of basic individual rights, direct effect, etc. The first type of constitutionalism I refer to in chapter 3 as "legalization" or "rule by law." It is normatively undemanding because under this definition, any legal system can be described as constitutional.
3. See for an application by the ICJ *Applicability of the Obligation to Arbitrate under Section 21 of the United Nations Headquarters Agreement of 26 June 1947*, Advisory Opinion, I.C.J. Reports 1988, p. 12, at 34.
4. We are not asking whether they could ever be relevant to questions of law and legal rule. Anything is potentially relevant under the right circumstances. So it is

no help to say that "[i]ndeed, as scholars of legal pluralism have long noted, 'not all the phenomena related to law and not all that are lawlike have their source in government"' (P. S. Berman 2006, 1170). This is a claim that no one contests. But there is a big leap from saying that lots of phenomena are *relevant or "related" to law* to saying that they should *count as law*. This is the indefensible move that broad-view legal pluralists unreflectively endorse.

5. Berman says, "First, it extricates international law scholars from fruitless debates about whether international law is really law at all, or which legal rules should be deemed 'legitimate.' As we have seen, legal pluralism provides international law scholars with a more comprehensive framework for conceptualizing the clash of normative communities in the modern world. This framework frees scholars from needing to differentiate so much between 'law' and 'non-law' or 'legitimate' and 'illegitimate' jurisdictional assertions. Such differentiations are less consequential in a pluralism context because the relevant question is the normative commitments of communities, not the formal status of those commitments" (2007, 323). But Berman simply moves the question one level up from "What is law?" to "What is a normative commitment?"
6. Pluralists are indeed tempted to reject the authority of law altogether. They claim, for example, that judges in nation-state courts are inevitably "people of violence" because their interpretations "kill off" competing normative assertions (P. Berman 2007, 304). Berman also says approvingly that pluralists "refused to give state law-making any more legitimacy or authority than other normative communities" (2007, 307). It seems that legal pluralists sometimes deny the distinctives of law as a system of social control and coordination altogether.
7. There are those who believe that distinct international law regimes, such as the WTO, are constitutionalized. I share Jeffrey Dunoff's skepticism that constitutional language is appropriate for those regimes (Dunoff 2009). But those who adopt the language of constitutionalism to describe international legal regimes do not claim that those constitutions are constitutions for the entirety of international law.
8. This tension has repeatedly come into play when, after extending its mandate to that of protecting human rights, the Security Council could always fall back on the excuse that any justified humanitarian intervention could undermine international peace. Indeed, the very willingness of the organs of the UN to call out catastrophic violations of human rights around the world has been limited by their need to work out the tension between a plurality of mandates, including maintaining international peace and stability and responding to evidence of massive harm. The politics of responding to the Rwandan genocide manifest this difficulty of navigating the terrain of a multidimensional mandate (Barnett 2003).
9. As Doyle shows, this inequality of power cemented by the rules is not limited to the Security Council. Due to a budgetary rule which relies on "functional consensus," eight members of the General Assembly which together cover 75% of the organization's budget "have a veto equivalent to the other 180 plus members" (Doyle 2009, 117–18).

INDEX